ON TV

William Walsh

keyhole
press

Keyhole Press
www.keyholepress.com

On TV

Cover design by Peter Cole.

ISBN: 979-8-218-40229-7

ON TV
William Walsh

In show business, the most important thing is sincerity.
And if you can fake that, you've got it made.

— George Burns

HERE'S JOHNNY

For thirty-four years on TV, Johnny carried me.
Johnny Carson carried me.

Hi-ho.
Heigh-ho.
O Magnificent One.
O Great Sage.
O Great Wind from the East.
O Large Loon of the West.
O Endlessly Nondescript One.
O Pseudo-insightful One.
O Giver of Fair Warning.
O Dean of Rare Divining.
O Source of All That Is Wet.
O Divine Spigot.
O Semisplendid One.
Hi-yooo.
Hi-yooo!
HI-YOOO!
Hi-yooo, my dear friend!
O Semidivine One.
O Blessed One.
I pray for that...

When I walked onto the first *Tonight Show,*
I walked into a thirty-year dream.

Thirty years of monologues. Thirty years of sketches. Thirty years of gags. Thirty years of questions and answers. Thirty years with the funniest man I ever knew.

Here, with Johnny's nervous blessing,
Is my answer to the question that

Drove this second banana bananas:

What was Johnny Carson really like?

Johnny was a shot of adrenaline. Johnny was smoking. Johnny was serious. Johnny was clearly bored. Johnny was still. Johnny was flying. Johnny was famous. Johnny was the greatest perfectionist. Johnny was enduring a bitter divorce. Johnny was a ventriloquist who knew how to throw his voice. Johnny was so competitive. Johnny was rare. Johnny was careful. Johnny was never able to suffer incompetents. Johnny was so cool. Johnny was an iceberg. Johnny was a better listener. Johnny was the best rebounder. Johnny was responsible. Johnny was unafraid. Johnny was a comedian, magician, writer, interviewer, and musician. Johnny was a comedian who blended Manhattan, Kansas with Manhattan, New York. Johnny was a man who glided smoothly between the broad and the subtle. Johnny was a happy man. Johnny was most alive when that camera light was on.

A prelude to Hi-yooo!

I began to prepare for my life with Johnny
when I was eight years old. I did (little) more
than lie on a rug and dream of microphones.
Dreaming since I was a small boy.
Dreaming the impossible dream.
Dreaming of midnight merriness.
My unwavering dream to be
America's greatest announcer.

Heeeeere's Johnny!

He had that nice slim build. He had no deep interest in food. He had self-confidence. He had an unerring instinct for how to get a laugh. He had the face of a fallen choirboy. He had keen radar for bad behavior. He had a special lewdness license.

Heeeeere's Johnny!

Johnny never said one word to me that wasn't sincere. Johnny never gave me a single piece of direction. Johnny never put his wife on the show. Johnny never talked to his guests before the show or during the commercial breaks. Johnny never felt comfortable. Johnny had the reputation for being cold and aloof.

Heeeeere's Johnny!

Johnny always managed to come up with just the right line. Johnny always knew exactly how far into blueness he could go. Johnny always made it funny for me, however, and probably just for me. Johnny always read newspapers to feed his monologue.

Heeeeere's Johnny!

A Tarantula. A tiger. A python slipping between Johnny's legs. The gibbon, the goat, the baby kangaroo, the baby ape, the marmoset, and the chimpanzee. He ran from a growling baby leopard and jumped into my arms. A good second banana knows how to catch the star.

> I always felt a little extra love
> for Johnny.
> Johnny and I were as close
> as two people can be.
> There was no faking what Johnny
> and I felt for each other.
>
> I arranged the first date
> with his third wife.
> That line came from Johnny,
> not one of his writers.

But Johnny. The impact of Johnny.

The last time I saw Johnny,
about a year before he died,
he *looked* like a million dollars.

Heeeeere's Johnny! Here's me.
Two grown men full of goo
Banana number two
Headed for deep doo.
And hilarity ensues.

Our days were one long lark.
The jollies never stopped.

It was one sweet dream.
So much applause.
Thick pork chops
With applesauce.

What a thoroughly decent man
Johnny Carson was.

You can't fake that on TV.

From *Here's Johnny!* by Ed McMahon. Rutledge Hill Press, 2005.

Our scripts averaged eighty-five pages while most one-hour shows are under fifty pages but still I wanted more: the longest monologue that had ever been done on TV.

I'M TALKING AS FAST AS I CAN

Firstly, hello. Hello. I just can't. Can't stop talking. Generally, just won't shut up. I'm not even sure what's going to come out of my mouth. Yada, yada, yada. Blah blah something. La la la la la la. Haha, yeah. Check me out. My mouth is moving on its own. And notice that no one was even talking about actors. As an actor, this made perfect sense. No, no. As an actor, this made no sense. Does that make sense? Needing to say every single word exactly as written. I still have to stop before I speak—speak words written for me. Acting is such a precarious profession. Actors actually don't get as much attention as you might think. But it's fun to pretend. There's a lid for every pot, they say. There's definitely an actor for every role. Even a small part. Oh, oh, look at me! New bike, same character! But seriously. I'm having déjà vu. Let me clear the air once and for all: Belly buttons are important. Just saying. Waiting for a better job or...my big break. I auditioned for the *Gilmore Girls*. I knew, from the very first time I read the script. I got the part, shot the pilot. It was exactly what I wanted. With regard to dialogue. The dialogue is delightful, that's our dialogue. Adrenaline-fueled dialogue. Clever dialogue. Dialogue to memorize. The most challenging dialogue was my favorite dialogue. Like—people talking over each other in a messy, authentic way. Our walk-and-talks so lengthy and complex. Just as thrilling and exhilarating as I'd imagined—quite literally a dream come true. A turning point. A tipping point. A plot point. The high point. At some point, you have to let it go. What's the point of living. Who knows, at this point. See what I did there? My voice. Reciting the lines in my head. I realize I'm holding my breath. I don't breathe properly. My voice sounded whispered, whispery, raspy. I'm, like, gasping for air—and my voice sounded thin, jumping up an octave. Whether you're saying it for real or just trying to get the part, say it loud and say it proud, which adds to the strangeness of it all. Fair to both sides is a sentence that has never before been written. I had trouble getting through the simple sentence. I can't even finish that sentence, run on—run or walk (run? don't run? I always forget). Negotiating. Renegotiation. AHAHAHAHA. There's almost nothing you can't say, unless you happen to have a strange block when it comes to saying filthy things. Not saying anything wasn't really working. Your character says dirty things. To say the least. Who can stop me saying whatever I want. When someone says something really nice. Something positive. Say something not so nice or say nothing. There's really nothing left to say. Deliver a long monologue. Okay, okay. A classical monologue, a contemporary monologue. I get weirdly shy. Speak up. Instead of shouting, babbling and drooling. Falling apart. Cut. It. Out. Apparently, I stopped listening. You can't talk. I'm like, I can't hear you. I don't want to. I don't want to. I don't want to. (Who can stop me?) I don't want to think the worst. Bogged down. Falling into place. I'm not saying either thing can't happen. There's a secret combination of elements that will make something that isn't easy a little easier. A sort of School of Fame where actors learn how to handle tricky situations. There's a sort of manic recognition that happens very rarely. There's a checked-out, drugged sort of look we get. I'm guessing this is preferable to them running away from you screaming, "Meth! Meth! So many years of meth!" Lengthy scripts getting longer. There were "talks." I did a lot of talking. You might want to skip this part. Full of sex and gossip. And full of tales. Full of happy smiling faces. Full of pretty dumdums. Full of sexual innuendo, and nudity. Full of X-rated movies. Full of junk food and a cake. Full of tattooed serial killer zombies. Talking about getting a tattoo. Prattling on about the possibility of getting a tattoo. A lot of tattoos on my upper butt area. Don't say: That sixth tattoo you got (isn't five enough?). I wanted exactly 152 tattoos. I started counting absolutely everything. How many steps I took. How many hours I slept. How many calories I ate. How many free margaritas I'd been given. How many pairs of sweat pants. How many followers I had on Facebook. And I realized I didn't want a tattoo anymore. The tattoo was, I realized, a perfect case of life being about the journey and not the destination. I'd been given the ultimate Fast Forward. In life, of course, there is no Fast Forward. Fast Forward doesn't even always work. I'm not a doctor, and I'll probably never play one on TV, because can you imagine? End the story. It's time. Such an odd conclusion to our epic adventure. I started to think about: Life. After the show. All that is to say I did indeed. Think about it. About her. Fast-talking Lorelai Gilmore. She talks very fast. Say something nice. Say something not so nice. Say something positive. Say something about being worried. That makes no sense. That makes no sense at all. Talk about *The Sound of Music*. Talk about how funny and perfect. Talk about planning a dinner. Talk about turning tables, and talk about all the long days and late nights. Talk for hours. Talk about what it was like, the *Gilmore Girls*. Roll my eyes and say, "Keep going, keep going, keep going." Whoa. That pretty much says it all, I guess. That makes no sense. Makes no sense at all, which makes perfect sense in a subtler sense—does that make sense? Make sense—in a new way? Talk about the long days. I'm talking about our final day. Tears. Hugs. Say thank you and look at each other, still a little dumbfounded. Sad to say goodbye. Say something like: Michael Jackson moonwalked on TV (that's the *Gilmore Girls*).

From *I'm Talking as Fast as I Can: From Gilmore Girls to Gilmore Girls (and Everything in Between)* by Lauren Graham. Ballantine Books, 2016.

After Jonah Winter's "Sestina: Bob"

I was only supposed to be on every other Tuesday...

ALL MY LIFE

— a sestina —

The fact that I was nominated for an Emmy
so many times. I was nominated for my first Emmy
in 1978, the inaugural year of the Daytime Emmy
Awards. Unfortunately, I didn't win the Emmy
that year. Someone else took home the Emmy.
I believed that one day I would win the Emmy.

A lot of people expressed the thought that I deserved the Emmy.
During the many years when I did not bring home an Emmy,
my happiness for who won was genuine. Winning an Emmy
has nothing to do with talent. Life is a cabaret. An Emmy
award is the extra icing on the cake. Until you win the Emmy,
you can't pull an Erica Kane, go up onstage and just take that Emmy.

The expression pulling a Susan Lucci, not winning the Emmy,
became part of our nation's vernacular. Don't talk about the Emmy
or any other award per se, obviously. Throughout my entire Emmy
journey—being Erica Kane on *All My Children*—that elusive Emmy
wasn't to be. A young girl dreaming of someday being on TV, at the Emmy
award show. A variation of the Cinderella story, losing the Emmy.

Applaud, laugh, cry. The process of being nominated for an Emmy
has evolved over the years. To be honest, winning the Emmy
was not something I thought about. Before I won my Emmy
for Best Actress, a friend suggested that since I didn't have an Emmy
we ought to name the new puppy Emmy. In the years that the Emmy
was mine to lose, everyone was talking about me not winning the Emmy.

Numb because I had lost so many times, I realized I needed the Emmy.
My mantra: Live and let live. The truth is, after my ninth Emmy
loss, I couldn't hear the name of the person who won. My tenth Emmy
nomination and loss. Nomination and loss. The whole Emmy
thing, my many nominations and losses. Eleven years without an Emmy!
Thirteen nominations. What does a person have to do to get an Emmy?

When I finally won, the fan appreciation was overwhelming. Emmy
was mine. It took me twenty-nine years to win my Emmy.
People say they are glad I finally got that Emmy. My Emmy.
I won. Outstanding lead actress. People felt impassioned about my Emmy.
As for me? I will continue doing what I love most—acting. My Emmy,
my long-awaited and treasured Emmy. SUSAN LUCCI won the Emmy.

This is Susan Lucci's Emmy. You can't take it away. I won the Emmy.
The streak is over. Indulge me while I shout my true feelings, at the Emmy
afterparty. Lots of hugs and kisses. I sure deserved it. I deserved the Emmy.

From *All My Life* by Susan Lucci. SL Enterprises, 2011.

YEAR OF YES
(A Disclaimer of Sorts)

I'm a liar
And I don't care
Who knows it

I make stuff up
All the time

True story

My brain
Naturally leans
In the direction
Of half truths

Because my brain

My brain
Bittersweet and sad
Oh my brain

My brain
Runs toward
Fiction

Like a flower
In the sun

Like writing
With my
Right hand

Like a bad habit
That feels good

The stuff I made up
Carried me from
The small bedroom
That I shared with my sister
To an Ivy League dorm room

All the way to Hollywood

I make stuff up
For a living

The storyteller
Inside me
Steps forward
And solves problems

My inner liar
Leaps in
To take over
My brain
To spin yarns

I call it Shondaland

Shondaland would
Literally not exist
Without the tales
The fiction
The stories
I've spun

Shondaland is a
Very real and
Very imaginary place

The imaginary
Land of Shonda
Has existed
Since I was eleven

Shondaland
Open
Creative
Happy

Shondaland
Quite literally
Saved my life

Flights of fancy
Make my motor run
Turn me on

Fabrication
Knitting yarns
Spinning tall tales

Making stuff up
Is responsible
For everything
I've done
Everything
I have

Figments of my imagination
Fill in the blank spaces
Paint over the nothingness

Because who
Doesn't want
To be on TV

In Shondaland
I wrap myself
In fiction

I write television shows
I make up characters
I create worlds in my head

Fiction is my job
Fiction is my jam
Fiction is everything

You think I'm kidding
I'm not kidding

It's true
It's clearly true

I lie
Artfully
Creatively

We all know what's true
I know what is true

The insides
Of my brain
Stories and images
Drifting
To places unknown

Thank you
Universe
You are pretty
And smart

So pretty
So smart

I like to make stuff up
And I like to lie

And it is true
Crazy but true

Don't stop dreaming
Until your dreams
Come true

That is the truth
I believe deeply

The truth
As I know it
As much as
A liar can know

From *Year of Yes* by Shonda Rhimes. Simon & Schuster, 2015.

MANKIND

Mankind on TV Mankind in the ring Mankind was a legendary performer in the ring Mankind could raise goosebumps on your arm Mankind on Pay-Per-View Mankind as the heel (bad guy) Mankind needed to be a heel Mankind had a heel persona Mankind was a great heel because he was so damn big Mankind was a great middle heel Mankind was a pudgy sneaky heel Mankind as the most hated heel Mankind as the number one heel Mankind as the hotter heel Mankind as the hottest heel Mankind is the story of a man who as a child dreamed of entertaining the masses inside a wrestling ring Mankind in the ring Mankind is really going to wrestle Mankind is wrestling with his buddies Mankind in a church basement Mankind was talking about the Kingdom of God—not the King Dome Mankind got a college education Mankind began throwing lefts and rights Mankind slapped his hands on the mat and came up shaking his fists Mankind consumed food of questionable origin Mankind absorbed through osmosis some understanding of what a referee does Mankind learned to work the mike Mankind is good television Mankind is the new hardcore Mankind wrestles his ass off Mankind does so many things that look inhuman Mankind would walk around with his Johnson blowing in the wind Mankind with his balls showing Mankind was talking to a girl with huge hooters Mankind was talking to her Mankind puzzled by boobs Mankind with his testicles in turmoil Mankind feels his nads Mankind had a sexual relationship with that woman Mankind went on a short run of rampant promiscuousness Mankind was talking too loud Mankind was talking way too much Mankind was talking about stacks of porno magazines Mankind was talking about bodily fluids Mankind was talking about considerable pain Mankind was talking with the Dream Mankind is hard enough Mankind used wrestling's most devastating move—sodomy Mankind had a reasonable shot at nailing that shit Mankind gets up every morning and looks in the mirror Mankind nodded and smiled blankly Mankind is an indictment of all—blame mankind for creating Mankind as a person Mankind is a MEW-TI-LAY-TOR Mankind rules Mankind is an insult Mankind laughed in your face Mankind grabbed a pair of chinos off the rack Mankind could throw down brews with the best of them Mankind is the best there ever was Mankind reflected a lack of humanity Mankind is the greatest clusterfuck Mankind put a twinkle in my eye and a bulge in my trousers Mankind gets a pedicure Mankind applies the mandible claw Mankind is the truth the whole truth and nothing but the truth—so help me Dude Mankind thought in-ring psychology was pretty simple Mankind is the norm Mankind had been thinking about psychology and criminal deviance—what makes a warped mind snap Mankind was a psychologist turned author Mankind was enthralled by how the plot was driven by some obscure mental illness Mankind is the possibility we could have been physically punished for Mankind is the little known and little exercised act of creating Mankind wanted to be on television Mankind was unique to television Mankind is the least sympathetic character in the business Mankind already had TV syndication Mankind depended on a more physical style and an episodic TV format Mankind began to lose matches on television with increasing regularity Mankind is punching downward with the point of the knuckles Mankind is the winner Mankind in the face of overwhelming odds succeeded Mankind makes you want to go out and dance a jig Mankind is the strangest Mankind was the worst natural wrestler Mankind was also the worst car singer Mankind was too loud Mankind was too heated Mankind broke three ribs Mankind clenching his fists Mankind backward off the top rope Mankind bumped backward to the mat Mankind on the mat with a rear chin lock Mankind heard a slap on the mat Mankind took a deep breath Mankind took a day off Mankind took a hell of a beating Mankind took a chokeslam Mankind took a hip toss Mankind backsuplexed into a table in perfect textbook form Mankind didn't have to rely on cheap violent stunts to get a pop out of the crowd Mankind knew what was coming next Mankind willingly obliged Mankind landed on the concrete Mankind hurtled through the audience Mankind rolls back into the ring Mankind gets the ten-count Mankind has been his own worst enemy sometimes Mankind is helped out of the ring by Francois Petit and referee Teddy Long Mankind's heel card had been played out Mankind fans were on their feet Mankind started yelling at his fans Mankind was bullshit Mankind really wasn't comfortable being a cowardly heel Mankind lost the belt Mankind was laughed right out of the ring Mankind shuffled away Mankind walked away Mankind from the ring to the graveyard Mankind too psychologically scarred to ever wrestle again Mankind left a trail of bloody handprints crawling away Mankind couldn't defeat the Undertaker Mankind put up a hell of a fight Mankind deserves a place in heaven Mankind goes to black and a video montage airs to the music of Jethro Tull's "Elegy" Mankind Mankind Mankind

---

From *Mankind: Have a Nice Day! A Tale of Blood and Sweatsocks* by Mick Foley. Regan Books, 1999.

I WAS THAT MASKED MAN

What was my dream?
To become a cowboy actor.

Where do cowboy actors work?
Hollywood. On TV.

Cowboy actor. Cowboy hero. Cowboy star.
Serial episodic. Serial cliffhangers.

A mysterious, masked man.
A figure of justice.

A bit of Robin Hood.
A dash of Zorro.

An unswerving champion
Of justice and fair play.
Bane of the outlaw.

Nicknamed Kimo Sabe,
Meaning trusty scout,
By his faithful, Indian
Companion, Tonto.

The thundering hoofbeats
Of the great horse, Silver.

The theme song.

Rossini's *William Tell* Overture.
Stirring music, galloping.

A brilliant white stallion.
A hand-carved saddle.
A stark landscape of craggy rocks.
Pausing at the summit of an incline,
Rearing, the horse stands on hind legs,
Paws at the air with its front hooves.
Hi Yo Silver! Away!

Opened with a bang.
Guns blazing. Dust flying.
A fiery horse with the
Speed of light.

Fifteen custom-made costumes.
Six pairs of hand-tooled boots.
Six special white Stetson hats.
Six shooter.

It always bothered me to see
Someone fire seven or eight
Shots from a six-shooter.

So I kept strict count.
Every time I fired my sixth
Bullet, I would reload.

Tonto and the Lone Ranger upheld the law.
Brought justice to the men in the black hats,
Rustlers, two-gun bankrobbers, bad men.
Led the fight for law and order in the West.

The Lone Ranger stood for everything
Good and decent in the West.

The epitome of a particular American archetype.
An exercise in Hollywood mythmaking.
Exciting Westerns filled with action.
Sweeping vistas, stunts, explosions.

Handling a firearm with panache.
Fast draws, fancy draws, gun twirling.
Over the shoulder shots. Tricks.

Silver bullets are the symbol
Of justice, fair play, and honesty.

Fabled crusader for law and order.
Moral upstanding, generous, honest, and
Patriotic. Uncommonly open and unguarded
For a man who wears a mask.

The Lone Ranger always wore the mask,
All the time, never letting anyone—except
Tonto—know his true identity,
The man behind the mask.

Superman. Batman.
Tarzan. Dick Tracy.
The Lone Ranger.

I *became* the Lone Ranger,
An American icon.
That American spirit.

Consistently noble.
Genuinely good.
Larger than life.

A cowboy has to have
That steely-eyed glare
In the close-up.

This blur between
Television persona
And private self.

I am only interested in playing
The Lone Ranger. Nothing else.
Anything else, I'm not interested.
I will only portray the Lone Ranger
In a show about the Lone Ranger.

Upright hero who would never shoot to kill,
Mysterious and valiant masked man...

A long, long ride into legend.
The masked rider never died.
The Lone Ranger rides.
Who was that masked man?
I was that masked man.

From *I Was That Masked Man* by Clayton Moore. Taylor Trade Publishing, 1996.

A PRIME-TIME LIFE

NARRATOR

He is AARON SPELLING, the most
Successful TV producer ever. One of
The most successful showmen of all time.

Dynasty, Melrose Place, Beverly Hills 90210,
Charlie's Angels, the Love Boat, Fantasy Island,
The Mod Squad, Hart to Hart.

The most prolific producer in history.

FADE IN: EXT. WESTERN PLAINS—DAY

AARON SPELLING (under MUSIC)

My father was a tailor.
His name was Spurling.

When he arrived at Ellis Island
The Officials didn't understand.
They renamed him Spelling.
(A BEAT)
Penniless. Jewish. Dallas, Texas.

CAMERA PANS from SHOT of a sky of blowing sand to kids running *to* something or *from* something.

AARON SPELLING (continues)

Every day I was chased home
From school, beaten up along
The way, by the bigoted sons
Of the tough cotton mill workers.

Most of it had to do with being Jewish.
There weren't a lot of Jews in Dallas.

I grew up thinking "Jewboy" was one word.

So many rednecks.

There wasn't a day I didn't get beaten up.

CUT TO: INT. BEDROOM (Nothing but a sagging mattress, stripped clean, a dresser filled with empty drawers.)

AARON SPELLING (continues)

I was always sick.

I made myself ill so I wouldn't
Have to walk to school.

Sickly little Aaron Spelling.

One day I went to bed
Thoroughly depressed
And couldn't find the energy
To get up.

For months I couldn't even walk.
I didn't go back to school for a year.

A doctor came to examine me.
The rabbi came to visit.

I made a decision to lie
In bed until I died.

Then my teacher came to see me.
She told me I was a good student,
And she had been impressed by the
Stories I told in class.

She handed me six books.

I discovered the wonders of reading...

And fell in love with the stories of
O. Henry, Mark Twain. Every
Book was an escape from my
World—a chance to visit wonderful,
Imaginary places.

I discovered that reading a book in a
Comfortable bed was better than

Skulking around the plains.

Reading became the primary activity of
My life, with movies running a close second.

My mother started taking me to movies on Saturdays,
My first inkling that there was this other world out
There.

I was such a big movie fan that I wrote to
All the stars to wish them Merry Christmas.

DISSOLVE TO: EXT. BATTLEGROUND DAY. HIGH SHOT.

NARRATOR
Fast-forward. World War II.

AARON SPELLING
I joined the Air Force on my eighteenth birthday.
My job was to function as a field correspondent
In France and Germany. I interviewed soldiers,
Sent their stories to their hometown newspapers.

CAMERA PULLS BACK:

AARON SPELLING (continues)
(typing...)
I submitted material to *Stars and Stripes.* Finally scored
With something called "Wacky-Khaki."
Your basic barracks-room humor.

I got into the Special Service, entertaining the troops.
I only weighed 118 pounds.
In Bavaria I received my Purple Heart.
(A BEAT)
Sniper got me.

CLOSE SHOT:

AARON SPELLING (continues)
They wanted to amputate two fingers.
I talked them out of it, telling them
I was a pianist. They sewed them up.

After the Army, I came home to Texas to attend
Southern Methodist University on the G.I. Bill.

At SMU I had a ball. I formed a comedy team. I got
Hired to direct plays for the Jewish community theater.
I got elected head cheerleader.

CUT TO: EXT. LA SKYLINE—NIGHT. CAMERA PANNING.

NARRATOR (under MUSIC)
Down on his luck in Hollywood...

AARON SPELLING
I rented a room at the Franklin Hotel
I was five steps below an apprentice actor.

I wanted to break into script writing.

Went to a bookshop on Hollywood Boulevard.
Bought a used script to learn proper form.
And went to work on my battered Royal.
(typing...)

Each night I would bang out spec scripts for TV shows.
I had written several one-act plays at SMU that had
Won awards. I figured writing TV shows would be a
Snap.

TOWARD CAMERA:

AARON SPELLING (continues)
I received a lot of rejection letters.

I looked at pictures of writers in Hollywood.
They were always smoking a pipe. I started
Smoking a pipe. I figured it helped make
You a better writer.

A pipe is the greatest crutch a writer has in the world.

I was able to let my imagination go wild.
I felt everything I wrote should say something.

CUT TO: EDTING ROOM. SERIES OF SHOTS. BLACK & WHITE

FOOTAGE ON TV SCREEN.

AARON SPELLING (voiceover)
...Trot out the clips of my acting appearances...

Like any actor, I went out on open calls.

Gunsmoke—I played a retarded Civil War soldier.
I Love Lucy—funny part of a gasoline attendant.
Willy—I played the dogcatcher.
Kismet—a beggar.
Dragnet—I played a retarded young man.

After seeing me like this, my then-wife Carolyn insisted
That I quit acting and stick to the typewriter.

FADE IN: INT. OFFICE NIGHT

AARON SPELLING
TV is a commercial medium.
On TV, shows follow a formula.

I had the surefire formula for success.

Come up with a plot.
Something with character.
A cute concept.

Ingenue. Great leading man.
Charge headfirst into conflict.
A conflict means there will be
A resolution to a problem or situation.

One-hour shows are built on four acts.
We set up the problem in act one and
Keep building on the problem until
We end with a resolution in act four.

In order to pay attention to detail,
You have to be able to pick the pepper
Out of the fly shit. Hit after hit.

EXTREME CLOSE SHOT

AARON SPELLING (quietly)
Chemistry is everything on TV. Bonding is everything.

CUT TO: EXT. HELICOPTER SHOT—MANSION. THEN TO THE LIBRARY
Quiet room. Big desk with a big chair.

AARON SPELLING (sunk down into chair)
Nepotism has become a four-letter word.

Tori is famous as TV's most prominent virgin.
The press gave her a hard time. She only got
The job on *90210* because of Daddy.

My wife never gets enough credit for my success.
She's a ditzy little blond but she's my real strength.
She taught me gentility. Her parents got over
Their distrust of me. Her father came to work for me.

Randy's the nonvisible member of the family.
When he was young, he used to make us laugh
By saying he wanted to be a "reducer" when
He grew up—his version of producer.

CUT TO: OFFICE—DAY

AARON SPELLING (into phone)
I am worried about portraying true stories on TV.

Violence does exist and sometimes it's necessary
To show it so kids can see how bad it is.

Speaking of the subject of TV violence, debated
Since the beginning of time: If a kid puts his pet
Caterpillar on the street, it's going to get squashed.
If you shoot it in a closeup, that's violence.

NARRATOR
Charlie's Angels was pure camp.
A glamourous, colorful fantasy.
Three sexy women, running around, solving cases.
None of them wears a bra. Talk about jiggle.

CUT TO:

AARON SPELLING
I'm King of the Jiggle.

BACK TO:

NARRATOR
Count up the many hours of
Television produced over the years.

The count is over 3,000 hours.
If you ran those shows for five
Hours a day, it would take more
Than 600 days to see them all.

Dynasty days—parties to watch
The show at country clubs.

College kids' *Melrose* parties every
Monday night. Hollywood players
Requested tapes of episodes they missed.

The appeal of *The Love Boat* was
Enormous for people who couldn't
Afford to go on a cruise.

CUT TO: EXT. A SUNSET STRIP HOT DOG STAND—NIGHT

A Parking lot Filled with sleek cars, fast cars, a convertible black Corvette, a motorcycle.

AARON SPELLING
I've produced over fifty TV series.
Nearly one hundred and fifty
Made-for-TV movies.

I was awarded a star on the
Hollywood Walk of Fame.
Something I never imagined could
Ever happen to me.

Hollywood, oh Hollywood!

When you're up they knock you.
When you're down they knock you.

NEW ANGLE—MOVING SHOT

Without dreams, there can be no reality.
Reality without dreams is a harsh world.
You can't keep your dreams to yourself
Because that's not sharing.

All my movies, my awards.

The inspiring rags-to-riches story of
A poor Jew from Texas.

It's like I boarded *The Love Boat*
And landed on *Fantasy Island*.
As if I visited *Fantasy Island* and
My fantasy became a reality.
(smiles)
What a picture!

CLICK. FREEZE FRAME.

THE END. FADE OUT & ROLL CREDITS

From *A Prime-Time Life* by Aaron Spelling. St. Martin's Press, 1996.

"The Great One. The Hustler. The serious actor. The biggest star on TV."

HOW SWEET IT IS

— A Foreword by Jackie Gleason —

It is now time for me to cop out.
An actor is a romanticist,
His vanity a worthless gem.
Vanity is an actor's courage. His
Self-deception thrives in flattery.
There is something noble about an
Actor's conceit—such a petty weapon.
With failure snapping at his heels,
His ego transforms failure into pride.
After a day of wishful drinking,
A puppy is stored in his heart.

My philosophy—play the melody.
Live, love, and lose gracefully.

From *How Sweet It Is* by James Bacon with a Foreword by Jackie Gleason. St. Martins, 1985.

Occasional appearances on TV weren't enough.
I wanted to be the one in control.
I wanted to be the one who knocked.

A LIFE IN PARTS

I'd been a working actor my entire adulthood.
Suddenly, in my fifties, I was a star.

Part of it is my nature.
Auditioning like a maniac for every part.
Cast me. Cast me. Cast me as the lead.
Smiles and nods at the audition.
I'd get the callback.
I could have gotten the part.
I'd lose the part to some other actor.
I didn't get the part. I got the part.
But, wait. What part?

Seinfeld superfans see me and shout, WHATLEYYYYYYY!
Tim Whatley, dentist to the stars.
Whatley converts to Judaism and starts making Jewish jokes.
Whatley! A dental Caligula, *Penthouse* magazines in his waiting room.

As Hal, I was strapped to the front of a city bus like a bicycle.
When something was wrong, Hal would show you what was wrong.
It made sense that he'd wear boys' underpants—tighty-whities.
Hal was just an overgrown boy, after all.
Hal was underdeveloped.
There wasn't a lot to Hal. But I was Hal.

Walt wasn't Hal.
Walter White was a Jekyll and Hyde character.
Walter White was alive. Walter White was evil.
I coveted that part. It was my part.
Foolish to think I had a shot at the part.
This part was so big. This was *the* part.
I began dreaming about this character, this Walter White.
I could see myself in the part. The right part.
Bryan Cranston?

The goofy dad from *Malcolm in the Middle*?
I was Walter White.
The part was mine. I knew it.
I was Walter White.
The part was mine!
I got the part. And what a part.
WALTER WHITE!
Irony isn't lost on Walter White.
People dress as Walter White for Halloween.
A critical turning point in the devolution of Walter White.
Leeching myself of Walter White.
I needed to let Walter White die.
I wasn't Walter White anymore.

I dreamed of a character.
A standard anxiety dream.
It was a dream but it wasn't.
Maybe it was a show on TV.

Study the character
Fully inhabit the character.
Get under the character's skin.
Find contradictions in a character.
Truly experiencing the pain of the character.
The character is honest and relatable.
The character hums and whistles a lot.
The character always leaned.

I imagine a character is outside of me.
Building a character is like building a house.
Once the character appears to me,
The character is no longer outside.

A character is driving off into the sunset.
I want the character to be me.
My character is driving away.
But my character is still there.

From *A Life in Parts* by Bryan Cranston. Scribner, 2016.

My job is on TV,
forecasting the weather.
I can tell you,
people just want to know
what to expect weatherwise
in their neck of the woods.

— Al Roker —

YOU LOOK SO MUCH BETTER IN PERSON

ALTRUISM #1
Assumptions Are NOT Your Friend

ALTRUISM #2
If You're Gonna Cry, Know How to Cry

ALTRUISM #3
Keep Your Day Job

ALTRUISM #4
Know the Cards and Play Your Best Hand

ALTRUISM #5
You Encounter More Personalities Than People

ALTRUISM #6
A Spoonful of Humor Helps Everything Go Down

ALTRUISM #7
Madness without a Reason Is Straight-Up Insanity

ALTRUISM #8
Get Your Piece of the Pie

ALTRUISM #9
Crying in Your Oatmeal-Soy-Almond Latte
Never Helps Anything

ALTRUISM #10
Get Up an Hour Before You Need To

ALTRUISM #11
Don't Goober Smoocher

ALTRUISM #12
Unless You're *Literally* the Sun,
Work Doesn't Revolve Around You

ALTRUISM #13
You Don't Need to Be the Top Banana

ALTRUISM #14
Don't Freak Out

ALTRUISM #15
Never Say No and Say Yes

ALTRUISM #16
Build Your Own A-Team

From *You Look So Much Better In Person* by Al Roker. Hachette Book Group, 2020.

CAPITAL GAINES

Is he as funny
in real life as
he is on TV?

The answer to that
is a resounding yes!

Funny in real life is
pretty different from
funny on TV.

I am a builder and a contractor.
I don't just play one on TV.

I'm a husband and father.
I'm a southern boy.

I'm a wild, obnoxious,
break-every-rule-in-the-book
risk taker.

I'm a pretty opinionated guy.
I'm a talker and could go on and on.

I'm positive.

I've always had the ability
to play things to the positive.
That mind-set.

For people with a winner mentality,
there's a positive waiting for you.

Every situation
has potential
for a positive
outcome.

My positive outlook
has blinded me to
plenty over the years.

I'll always shoot you straight.

I'm a firm believer
that figuring things
out on your own
is more effective
than being given
something on
a silver platter.

Things that make my head a bit dizzy:

Hammering, heights, melodrama, shiplap (ship-what?), blood, drywall, lawyers, football coaches, the blazing hot sun (quite literally the sun is hot), English, math.

That said, I'd like to be
your coach and have
you on my team!
We can hammer out
the possibilities together.

Really special things about Chip Carter Gaines:

Chip was born in Albuquerque, New Mexico.
Chip had a horse. Chip became a true cowboy.
Chip handles construction. Chip makes.
Chip prefers to work.
Chip Gaines, Builder.
Chip is an entrepreneur by nature.
Chip wouldn't take no for an answer.
Chip loves life. Chip remembers.
Chip is a good man. Chip is a saint.

Chip specializes in making
the impossible possible.
Chip talks about how life isn't
about arriving; it's what
happens on the way.

"CHIP! CHIP! CHIP! CHIP! CHIP!
"CHIP! CHIP! CHIP! CHIP!
"CHIP! CHIP! CHIP!
"CHIP! CHIP!"

A hot cable
TV show about
the ups and downs
of designing and
renovating homes.
We don't use a hair
and makeup or
wardrobe team
like most of our
counterparts
on TV.

We underdoggers love
to see the unexpected
prevail—and I love my face!

We are crystal clear
on the differences
in our strengths.

We specifically feel like
God has initiated
something.

We expect God
to show up
and he (sic) does—over
and over again.

Do I want a safe, comfortable, and easy life?
Or do I want my days to matter?

Praying and seeking God.
Praying and seeking God.

Why did God pick me of all people?
Maybe—God forbid—I was just normal.

God-given abilities.
God-given strengths.
God-given gifts.
God-given talent.
God-sized risk.

Ultimately, I know
God's Plan B
has been infinitely
greater than
my Plan A.

God's plan since the very beginning.
That's God's own truth.

Knowing that God will be right there with me.
God somehow uses that for my good too.
It almost seems nonsensical to walk away
from this miraculous gift from God,

Walking closely with God. Trusting God.

We have seen the hands of God.
God had given us this gift

God's grace lasts as long as it is required.
But any gift God has for me, I'm taking it.

The fact that something is from God does not
mean it's forever. The Lord gives, remember,
and the Lord takes away.

God has a way of proving to us
just how little control we have
over things.

I have seen the burden God
has laid on the human race.

Yet no one can fathom what God
has done from beginning to end.

Toil—this is the gift of God.

A *job* is something you do for money.

Your life's *work* is done for a bigger purpose,
to fulfill a calling or a dream.

Making money feels good—a ton of money.

God in a way. From God. Thank God.

> One of the things I've learned
> about God is that he (sic) loves
> to obliterate the boxes we put
> him (sic) in.
>
> That's who we are.
> That's what we do.
> That's how we think.
>
> We are children of God—the whole lot of us.
>
> And oh, yes—we got to go on TV!

From *Capital Gaines*, by Chip Gaines, W Publishing Group, 2017.

MY SQUIRREL DAYS

Reader I must tell you
much of this
the squirrel wrote

My memory is fuzzy

I was young and confused
wanted to be anyone
but me

I lived my life
like I was
a cartoon character

I would occasionally test God
God existed
all right

I began communing
with an overweight squirrel
in a treehouse in my backyard

I named her Natalie

Natalie was different from me

Natalie had a way about her

She had a tail
I did not

There was something different
about her

She liked food
I wanted her to like me

I decided to feed Natalie

I sought refuge among the animals
a wannabe squirrel whisperer

I started talking less
squeaking more

I had an ability
to communicate
with wildlife

My new identity hit me
like a ton of monkey dung

I too was an animal
a skittish pony
but with human legs

I have powerful quads
with which I'm well-pleased

I found myself settling deeper and deeper
into the squirrel community

Patch had a small patch of white on his back
Ears had unusually large ears
Brownish was a little more brown than gray
Tiny was very small
Squirrels HAHAHAHAHAHAHAHAHA
lol

Other squirrels would travel together
in scampering groups
of two or three

Natalie was always alone
She didn't climb trees
Her pace was hardly a scamper
Hers was more of a labored plod
Natalie moved at her own pace
and she was always eating

Natalie lived her life
one plunk at a time

Natalie didn't	allow time to dictate her life
She wasn't She wasn't	the class clown a showboat
She was just	an obese squirrel trying to get through the day
Natalie wanted	to try improv to put on shows together
This made	her infinitely more mysterious than the other squirrels
We spent time	improvising scenes getting to know each other
It was surreal	seeing squirrels in the audience and fruit bats too
I learned a lot	from Natalie
I quickly learned	that listening and responding formed the core of improv
Natalie was	one of the greatest improvisers of all time
Yes	and
I was	getting so good at improvising it was almost funny
I made up	in pluck what I lacked in natural ability
Improv	was everything

I wanted to be a star

I wanted to perform for
a human audience
an audience of
kind and normal people

The world of improv beckoned me

I thought my life could be
a Lifetime movie
on TV

We were an improv team
Natalie and me

She was my first improv partner

Sketch ideas flittered and fluttered about

I decided to devote more time
to my improv

With Natalie I was an
amped up version
of myself

I never broke eye contact with Natalie

I know you I whispered

Natalie was just an obese squirrel
trying to make it through the day

I was just a field-hockey-dropout-turned-improviser

I dreamed about the ImprovOlympics
The Upright Citizen's Brigade
Second City
SNL

In the world of show business
it's every squirrel
for herself

So many	auditions
I landed	my first job on TV and not just any show a really good TV show
I owe it all	to Natalie
One squirrel	a fairly overweight squirrel made me laugh made me think made me strong
Natalie made me	the improviser that I am today
I will never forget	my squirrel days

From *My Squirrel Days* by Ellie Kemper. Scribner, 2019.

Viewers subscribe to the
All-blondes-on-TV-look-alike theory.

ANCHORWOMAN

As soon as I heard my voice
On the airwaves, my destiny
Was fixed.

I wanted to be an anchorwoman.
A new term for a new time.

Dubbed NBC's Golden Girl.
Called reporter by courtesy only.

Fame, fortune.
A glamorous life.
Paid a lot of money
For looking pretty
And reading words
On television.

I'm Jessica Savitch.
I was never very happy.

A poem about a woman
Who climbs a mountain
To see the view.
At the end of the day
She realizes
She passed the top
Because the rest of the way
Was downhill.

Looks should neither
Attract nor distract.

A reporter's appearance
Should be just pleasant enough
To disregard.

Put me on camera.
She reads well.
But can she report?

> You're at a desk
> You've got a script
> You face two cameras
> And a TelePrompter
> And you do the news.

I'm Jessica Savitch.
No such person existed.

I very much wanted to be
Accepted by my peers,
To be considered
A serious journalist.

It is possible to be
Simultaneously
Aggressive and feminine.

News is what happens
When individuals act,
Interact, and react in a
Bigger-than-life-way.

Pocket mirrors, nail files, lipsticks,
Powder puffs—all manner of feminine
Accoutrements.

Fallen victim to chauvinistic clichés.
The first of my bubbles burst.

Looks are part and parcel of the industry.
I decided to quit apologizing for my looks.

I learned to read three wire service
Versions of a story and cull them down,
Shaping them into my own style.

Shorter is always better.
Think it out in your mouth.
A sentence that reads well
Might not speak well.

I would call myself Jethica Thavitch
Until I was well into my teens.

A starry-eyed little girl.
Doesn't know anything.
That stupid little girl.

Find a capacity to disregard criticism.
Rid myself of the vestiges of a lateral lisp.

I was an unwitting
Pioneer in my field.

Male-only, old-boy
Bastion of newscasters.

You would think
I lived between
Commercials.

I was perhaps too insecure,
Skittish and nervous.
I was motivated by fear.

I was categorized as a beginner,
Pigeonholed as a glossy blond
A newsreader hired to dress the set.

Promoted, hyped, used, abused,
And propelled into stardom.

A meteoric rise to stardom.
Only to have it all end.

What do you hide
When everything is
Hanging out?
Your face.

For every two minutes of glamour
There are eight hours of hard work.

Gracious characteristics.
Psychotic ramblings.
Willing to work for a small salary.
I spilled out all my frustrations.

> Fans want stars to be who
> You are in (their) fantasies.

Jessica Savitch?
The Jessica Savitch?

Celebrities are made vulnerable
When they begin to believe
They are valued for themselves
And not for what they do,
When they begin to believe
The power is theirs to keep
And not just on loan.

> You do have a definite presence on screen.
> But you look like an ordinary person!
> And to a degree you do.

A few glasses of champagne
And the room began to sway,
Undulating around me
In a dizzying blur.

Preoccupied and rather sad.

> You can get someone to wear
> A Dan Rather sweater and do
> A Dan Rather delivery, but you
> Won't have Dan Rather.

An anchorwoman has two choices of men;
Those who date her because of her job, and
Those who date her in spite of her job.

In our culture, saying, I have to work late
Is another way of saying, I'm not interested.

We have indeed come a long way
If we can take our jobs but not ourselves
Seriously.

Do you think you would be where
You are if you weren't pretty?

The intimate relationship
Built up over time
Between an anchor
And the viewers.

The news anchor is exactly that—
An anchor, a center, a focus.
The modern-day tribal experience
Of our mobile society.

We don't just shoot our heroes.
We often destroy them
By setting up unrealistic
Expectations.

An extra drink at the bar.
Hangover recovery.

News, sports, and weather.

I was tired—too tired
To make reasonable decisions.

No matter how many goals
You have achieved
You must set your sights
On a higher one.

There are two dangers in life:
One is not getting what you want;
The other is getting it.

I'm Jessica Savitch.
I was on television.

Somewhere between
The dream and a
Harsher reality.

On-air a second can seem like a year.
Dumbly staring into the camera.
A bad dream. Smile. Gritted teeth.

The prompter pages were out of order.
The TelePrompTer could not be fixed.

It was time to sign off.

From *Anchorwoman* by Jessica Savitch. G.P Putnam & Sons, 1982.

I AM THE NEW BLACK

I.
The version of me you see on TV
Is a pretty happy guy, isn't he?

You could say that I've grown up on TV.
I definitely went from a boy to a man on TV.

What can I say?

I am the new black.

The new black is impossible
To define—and so am I.

Black isn't the absence of color,
It's the presence of all color.

That's why I'm the new black.

The new black is something that
Our American society needs
At every level because

The new black
Isn't about race,
It's about *trying*.

Being the new black means
You can get there if you try.

In this era of the new black,
You have to try because
There's no more excuses.

I might go down in history
As the first black man
Lynched by black people.

Racism definitely exists,
And the new black knows this,

Just like the new black knows
That now is the time to stand up.

The truth is that, like the new black,
I'm impossible to define.

Because I am the new black.

I am the new black.

II.
You laugh when you see me on TV.

People ask me how I got so funny.

    keep me *real*
    let me improvise
    I'm still me

When you're on top, it's amazing
How many old friends you have.

I was at a real physical low point.
Suffering from my own neglect.

Stand up was all I had going.

I've seen so many of the black males
I grew up with end up dead or in prison.

    never thought
    it would be
    okay for me
    to break character

I have friends who are black, white,
Purple, gay, straight, Martian,
Yellow, old, and young.

Give this black man his trophy.

I don't mean to speak for all black Americans.
Black people might be proud of their own.

Whenever a black comedian achieves
A certain level of success, they get asked
About racism in the entertainment industry.

I'll tell you something—

After being on *SNL* for seven years,
The people I met knew who I was
And thought they knew shit about me.

There have never been a lot of black guys on *SNL*.

At *SNL* we were all definitely family.

When I'm onstage
Or on TV
I might be
The biggest clown
You ever saw
But when I'm not,
I like my privacy.

When someone like me,
A guy from the neighborhood
Who is on TV, gets popped
For a DUI, every single
Motherfucker on the block
Is gonna be talking about it.

I believe that even today,
On mainstream shows,
Outside of the urban television market,
Black people on TV
Are held to a higher standard.

You probably don't understand
What's funny about my funny.

The parts of me
That make you laugh
When you see me
On TV.

III.
BLACK COMEDY IS: REDD FOXX
BLACK COMEDY IS: RICHARD PRYOR
BLACK COMEDY IS: EDDIE MURPHY
BLACK COMEDY IS: DEF COMEDY JAM
BLACK COMEDY IS: THE 90s MARRIAGE OF HIP-HOP AND COMEDY
BLACK COMEDY IS: THE WORD MOTHERFUCKER

IV.
Not just a funny insult but a funny
Insult delivered in an unexpected way.

That's cool with me. I'm happy about that.
Black people dance well because we start early.

White people? They don't know what it's like to be black!

I don't pay attention
To boundaries. I go
Wherever the fuck
I want to go.

One of my memories
Was the day I got lost
At the Bronx Zoo when
I was nine years old.
I saw all the animals.

I had wandered away
From my family.
It took me hours
To realize I was lost.

That scared me to death.
I was lost, but now I'm found.
Learning what I can,
Just like I did when I was kid.

You need to pray.
You need to pray to
Whatever God you
Believe in. You have to.

Pull all your mental energy

Into achieving your goal.

I thank God for my gift of funny.

If God gives you a talent,
You've got to honor it
By giving it your undivided
Attention. I'm still a good
Person and I thank God
For that—He's working
With me on it. Every day
I thank God for what I have
because I'm lucky to be alive.

I've lived. I've lost.
I've strived. I've survived.
I've come a long way.
I've achieved a lot.
I've learned a lot about myself.
I've climbed a mountain.
I've come through it all.

Here I am, against all odds,
Still going strong on TV.

From *I am the New Black* by Tracy Morgan. Spiegel & Grau, 2009.

CALL ME LUMPY

They all knew I was on TV.
Everyone knows Lumpy.
Everyone in the world.

I am just...so lucky. I just happened.
I have always been right on time.

Whoever's pulling the strings up there,
I am one of his favorite puppets.

I am blessed to be part of the Beaver family.

I was a regular on the show.
A nice and pleasant show.
Good, clean entertainment.

Neat and neat-o became part of the personality
Of "Leave it to Beaver." Neat. I felt good using the word.

Remember that time you lost your haircut money?
The time you ordered something from a catalogue
Without mom and dad's permission?

This is not real life. This is comedy.

I had the greatest childhood anyone could ever want.
The greatest adolescence. My whole life, you could
Call me Lucky instead of Lumpy.

Behind the Lumpy innocent facade
Was a wild child inside me about
To get out. And the more I passed
From being a child, the wilder he got.

Drag racing got popular.
I raced. You bet I did.
I raced my Corvette.

My Corvette was painted regal turquoise.
It had black leather interior. It was fuel-injected.

Corvettes ruled.
Ask the Beach Boys.
Ask Jan and Dean.
The Ripcords.
Everything was Corvettes.
They all sang about them.

And then came the sexual revolution.
I was at the very center of it.
All it was, was havin' fun.
I was hoggin' it up.

And, oh, God, did I have fun.
I loved being out among 'em.
The sex was very communal.

Lots of toga parties.
Lots of towel parties.
Lots of poker and liquor.

Beavers have always been good to me,
In more ways than one. I used to take out
A lot cheap girls in the hopes that they
Would go to bed with me.

But they weren't "conquests" to me.
I always liked to think that I left
All those girls a little bit happier
For the experience.

If the sex jokes were lame, the sex wasn't.
Ha, ha. Hey, what do you want from me?
It's supposed to be sophomoric humor.

Sex was always the dessert. The cherry on top.
Sex set the undertone and overtones to each day.

We didn't have to go
Looking for girls.
Girls found us
Wherever we went.

Starlets and harlots.
Girls from high school.
College girls. Sure.

I loved playing poker.
Slots. Blackjack. Craps tables.
I loved making money.
Money was the way you kept score.

Pretty good parlay, huh?

When you do it right, there is no gamble
Involved in poker. It is the one game
At the casinos that is largely technique.
But I was a lucky gambler. Extremely lucky.

Becoming a professional poker player.
Becoming a great financial analyst.
It was the same thing.

I make money, hopefully, by investing
My clients' money in a proper way.
I do not make my money by walking up
To a craps table and trying to hit sevens.

> Lumpy, Lumpy, dumb as an ox.
> Loudmouthed fat kid.
> Derogatory words. Lumpy.
> A schmuck, a dullard, a dimwit.
> A nerd. A putz. Peckerhead.

I am the opposite of that. I am the
Antithesis in every way, shape, and form.

Lumpy is the man.

I believe in Barbara and Hugh and
Ward and June and Tony and Wally and
Kenny and Eddie and Jerry and the Beaver.
I believe in Beaver.

On the show whenever anyone called
Clarence Rutherford by his nickname
He always replied, irritably in that
Whiny voice of his, Don't call me Lumpy.

But I say, Call me Lumpy.

I say it proudly, Call me Lumpy all you want.
I am happy that the name Lumpy stuck
With me all these years. Happy.

I am the luckiest man alive.
The Lumpy character endured.
Call me Lumpy any time at all.

From *Call Me Lumpy* by Frank Bank. Addax Publishing, 1997

I STOOGED TO CONQUER

— a pantoum —

After the release of our shorts on TV
There wasn't a laugh in me
Slap-stick off-color jokes
Clobbering Larry, Shemp, and Curly

There wasn't a laugh in me
Repeating our act
Clobbering Larry, Shemp, and Curly
Getting solid laughs but a far cry from the old days

Repeating our act
Slap-stick off-color jokes
Getting solid laughs but a far cry from the old days
After the release of our shorts on TV

From *I Stooged to Conquer* by Moe Howard. Citadel Press, 1977.

THIS IS YOUR CAPTAIN SPEAKING

I've been a Captain! It's so much more
    than what you see on TV.
I emanated a sense of authority when
    I put that uniform on.

Even though I was only acting.

If you put a guy in a uniform,
    people will listen to him more
    than if he's in street clothes.

The uniform itself is what did it.

Captain Merrill Stubing.

The Captain had originally been conceived
    as a stern, authoritative boss—but I saw
    him as something different.

I saw him as a leader: the kind of guy who
    cares deeply about his crew, and his
    passengers, and who takes responsibility
    for his crew and passengers in a loving
    way.

In a sense, Merrill Stubing would become
    more of a father figure in my hands.

Everybody loved the Captain.
    Such a nice guy on TV.

I'm the Captain of *The Love Boat,*
    a cruise ship.

— o —

The story of *The Love Boat* from day one:
    the critics hated us; the people loved us.

The people kept us on the air.

A Captain is a role of authority,
a role that's looked up to. It's
a fatherly figure, and that in
and of itself is different than
playing almost any other
type of role on TV.

God gave me that role.

God knows he (sic) is the
Captain of my world.

I think God was pushing me toward
that role my entire life. I played the
Captain of the *Pinafore* in a Gilbert &
Sullivan production in high school.

Captain Applejack.
Operation Petticoat.
McHale's Navy.
The Love Boat.

I think he (sic) gave me the role of the Captain
so that I could serve as a stand-in "Captain"
to a few people here on earth—to help
guide them on their way into his (sic) arms.

I'm doing God's work, as his (sic) ambassador.

Putting lessons in a TV show isn't
easy without sounding corny.

I looooooved our messages—because we
covered them with cotton candy.

Captain Stubing was a single guy.

The writers didn't want him to seem loveless.
One storyline they did a flashback.

His younger days...a beautiful girl...a warm
scene in front of a fireplace...very lovey-
dovey...and he said to this girl, Will
you marry me? She looked at him
and replied, On one condition...
it's either me or the sea.

He couldn't do it. The Captain couldn't
quit his job. His first love was
being the Captain. That's why
he was still a bachelor.

Whether you feel like your ship is
setting sail or sinking, you will be
in good hands with *this* Captain.

Put the Captain on a boat!

I never could have imagined that someday
I would be the Captain of my own show,
anchoring a TV series.

I never imagined I would travel
all over the world!

I've been a Captain! It's so much more
than what you see on TV...

From *This is Your Captain Speaking* by Gavin MacLeod. Thomas, 2013.

CONFESSIONS OF A PRAIRIE BITCH

at age twelve
I was cast
as one of the
biggest brats
on TV

I am
commonly
known
as the
Prairie Bitch

Nellie Oleson

a bitch
a horrible
wretched
scheming
evil
lying
manipulative
selfish brat
whose narcissism
and hostility
toward others
knew no bounds

a girl who millions
of people all over
the world had
grown to hate
but a girl I
grew to love

Little House on the Prairie
made you feel good
made you appreciate
what you had and
stop bitching about
what you didn't

those Ingalls girls
didn't have a penny
to buy a slate pencil

that's poor

I did not read the
Little House books

Laura Ingalls Wilder
Mary and Carrie
Charles and Caroline
Almanzo and Adam
Miss. Beadle
a brother called Willie
and me, Nellie Oleson

I *looked*
like a nice
little girl
but dainty
was not
my thing

I did not join
the Brownies
and I never
became
a Girl Scout

here's a dark thought
imagine people telling
you that you're beautiful
and fabulous and that
they love you
but you know
that they've
never seen
the *real* you

I am repeatedly
held to account
for the actions of
a fictitious character

boo-hoo-hoo
my teacher hates
me because I'm
a child star

but I am happy
I was "the Nellie"
not just happy
proud and grateful

I wanted to be on TV

by making me a bitch
you have given me
the freedom
to say and do
things I couldn't
do if I was
"a nice girl"
with some
sort of stupid
goody-two-shoes
image to keep up

things that require courage
things that require balls
things that need to be done

by making me
a bitch
you freed me
from the
trite
sexist
bourgeois
prison
of "likeability"

any idiot
can be liked

it takes talent
to scare the
crap out of
people

fight back
be bold
daring
determined
down-right
sneaky

if enjoying that
as much as I do
makes me a bitch
well goody

being marked
a bitch for life
on TV
is the best thing
that ever
happened
to me

I owe it all to the
little bitch on the prairie

all I can say is
thank you

I learned this
lesson on TV

From *Confessions of a Prairie Bitch* by Alison Arngrim. HarperCollins, 2010.

"After a day of family-television dialogue, I'd release my demons onstage."

DIRTY DADDY

The whole show for me was a Jekyll and Hyde experience. The good and the bad. The sweetly neurotic Danny Tanner on *Full House*. The comedy of

Bob Saget. The good and the bad. The tenor of my comedy, raunchy stand-up routines, sick jokes, dick jokes. Constant dick jokes. Too many dick jokes, just

riffing. Danny Tanner, was the personification of family-friendly. Bob Saget was a huge asshole! The good and the bad. I was a good person for hundreds

of millions of people on TV. Unless cameras were rolling, I pretty much was not Danny Tanner. The good and the bad. I was careful about my

language—this helped me get on television. But ever since I can remember, I was always trying to look up dresses. I was a dirty little bastard. The good

and the bad. We do seem to be getting farther away from the purity and intended beauty of *Full House*. Uncle Jesse and Joey. The good and the bad.

D. J. and Stephanie. The twins. The good and the bad. Truth is, behind the scenes it was often as sweet and gooey, family-wise, as it was on the air. The

good and the bad. Conceived as a guy who loved his kids more than anything, Danny Tanner was a hugger and a neurotic compulsive cleaner.

Oh, Danny Tanner. He was a man who was more than a man. He was a widower, full of woe. He was a woe-man. The good and the bad. When you

see me on TV and it's on cable, turn off the sound. I look like I'm saying nice stuff when the sound's off. Seriously, who gives a shit about Bob Saget?

From *Dirty Daddy: The Chronicles of a Family Man Turned Filthy Comedian*, by Bob Saget. It Books, 2014.

Pioneers, the original VJs,
Alan, J. J., Mark, Martha, and Nina.
Together, they were a five-headed Virgil
Taking us through MTV's Inferno.

VJ

Welcome to Your Life

Step Right Up and Don't Be Shy

There's Always Something Happening and It's Usually Quite Loud

Let's Make Lots of Money

Don't Talk to Strangers

Sometimes You Tell the Day by the Bottle That You Drink

Ain't Nothing Gonna Break My Stride

Here in My Car, I Feel Safest of All

I Hope That When This Issue's Gone, I'll See You When Your Clothes Are On

I'm a Cool Rocking Daddy in the U.S.A.

Hot in the City

Throw Your Arms Around the World at Christmastime

Got My Back Against the Record Machine

Changes Come Around Real Soon, Make Us Women and Men

Take My Tears and That's Not Nearly All

I'll Kick You Out of My Home If You Don't Cut That Hair

And Now You Find Yourself in '82

I Know There's Something Going On

Things Can Only Get Better

I Spend My Cash on Looking Flash and Grabbing Your Attention

She's Precocious and She Knows Just What It Takes to Make a Pro Blush

They Told Him Don't You Ever Come 'Round Here

You Must Be My Lucky Star

I Might Like You Better If We Slept Together

Every Time I Think of You, I Always Catch My Breath

That's My Soul Up There

I've Seen You on the Beach and I've Seen You on TV

I Want to Be the One to Walk in the Sun

You Play the Guitar on the MTV

You May Find Yourself in a Beautiful House with a Beautiful Wife

My Beacon's Been Moved Under Moon and Star

Jokerman Dance to the Nightingale Tune

The Kids in America

I Always Feel Like Somebody's Watching Me

What a Pity You Don't Understand

I Said to the Man, Are You Trying to Tempt Me?

I Was There to Match My Intellect on National TV

There Comes a Time When We Heed a Certain Call

Love Is a Battlefield

I Guess I Should Have Known by the Way You Parked Your Car Sideways
That It Wouldn't Last

The Kid Is Hot Tonight

I Don't Wanna Lose Your Love Tonight

The Five Years We Have Had Have Been Such Good Times

The Party Boys Call the Kremlin

I'm a Man Who Doesn't Know How to Sell a Contradiction

We'll Be Moving on and Singing That Same Old Song

Every Now and Then I Get a Little Bit Nervous
That the Best of All the Years Have Gone By

After the Fire, the Fire Still Burns

Don't You Forget about Me

We Can't Rewind, We've Gone Too Far

From *VJ: The Unplugged Adventures of MTV's First Wave*, by Nina Blackwood, Mark Goodman, Alan Hunter, Martha Quinn, and Gavin Edwards. Atria Books, 2013.

EVERY DAY I FIGHT

You have cancer.
The initial hit
Of those words.

Like any great opponent
Cancer is in your face.

When cancer storms into your life
You have a choice: fight or curl up
And just be a cancer patient.

I know how to fight.
I know how to punch.
I know how to kick.

You focus on the fight
Not on the fright.
You don't give up.

Cancer fighter had become
The way I thought of myself.

Bound and determined
To beat cancer. To win.

When you have cancer
You scour the Internet.
You find a lot of negativity.

Seemingly every cancer story
On the Internet is about dying.

My boys were like, Man, you scared?
I was like, Damn right I'm scared.

Headline: ESPN Anchor's Private Battle with Cancer Becomes a Public One

Because I'm on TV
People expect me
To be an extrovert.

A badass on TV
Look tough on TV.
Cancer fighter.

No doubt makeup could
Cover up the scars
When I'm on TV.

This warrior cancer guy.
Superman cancer fighter.
A badass who kicks ass.

It wasn't just that I'm on TV
Though that's part of it.

Wearing a black 'Every Day I Fight' T-shirt.
Gray T-shirt reads 'Fuck Cancer #stustrong
In black lettering. T-shirts for everyone.

Cancer turns
The old cliché
On its head.

It can kill you *and*
Make you stronger
At the same time.

What hits home
Is just how much
You are forever changed
Once you have cancer.

Cancer robs you
Of the ability
To grow old.

You don't beat cancer just by living.
You beat cancer by *how* you live.

People with cancer are fighters.
They are survivors.

The problem is one of language.
We have a tendency to foist
Heroism upon people with cancer.

Cancer tried to keep me.
That's what cancer does.

My voice droned:
I have cancer.
I'm scared.
I'm going to die.
I hate cancer.

Playing the cancer card.
Warrior or victim.
The way I thought of myself.

I was still
Doing my thing
At the gym.

I'm an every-day guy.
Even with cancer.
I'm an every-day guy.

A never-give-up guy.
Bound and determined
To beat cancer.

Headline: ESPN Anchor Stuart Scott Refuses to Let Cancer Win

Before ESPN,
I won an award
For editing together
Orlando Magic highlights
To C+C Music Factory's
'Everybody Dance Now.'

As a broadcaster on ESPN
I brought the attitude
Of hip-hop to *SportsCenter*.

I learned not to try to be
Something that I'm not.

Very few people pay attention
To good writing on TV.
Even in my earliest days,
I knew that I could write.

I'm not talking about
Writing the King's English,
Using ten-karat words.

I'm talking about writing
That doesn't sound like writing.

I'm talking about writing
That sounds like you're
Having a conversation.

Funny, what cancer gives you.
It makes you more open, vulnerable.

Laughing and crying—the
Literal definition of having cancer.
This is what cancer does.

Cancer is relentless.
Trying to beat this thing.
What an SOB cancer is.

Waking up
With a catheter
In my manhood.

If catheters are playing
The Ku Klux Klan
In a football game,
I'm rooting for the Klan.

Cancer's this big bad fifty-foot monster
And you feel like you're fighting by yourself.

The cancer fight.
Its relentlessness
Bears down on you,
Shakes your
Self-assuredness.

I was being
What I'd said
I wouldn't be,
Nothing but
A cancer patient.

No energy.
No will.
Shadowboxing.

Thinking about that day
When the *Lawd* comes
To take me. Amen, brotha.

Headline: The Most Moving Thing About Stuart Scott's Speech at the ESPYs.

Because I'm on TV
My fight against cancer
Was a public event.

I'm a public figure.
I have a public job.
I'm battling cancer.

Hopefully I'm inspiring.

I started the day
Hating cancer
With a passion
And I ended it
With love
Bursting outta me.

That's what cancer does.
It messes with you.
But it also makes
Your love much bigger.

That night at the ESPYs.

Don't give up.
Don't ever give up.
That's the key to life.

Life is hard.
Life is a trip.
Life's too short.

When you die,
It does not mean
That you lose.

Don't. Give. Up.
Think of me.
We talked sports
For a little while.

From *Every Day I Fight* by Stuart Scott. Blue Rider Press, 2015.

HOLD THE ROSES

…Joy was working on TV
I worked with some very talented and wonderful people
Dick Van Dyke, thank God for him
Bill Corey, a real honest-to-God cowboy
Thank God for Bill Corey
Morey Amsterdam, Bless him
Carl Reiner, a blessing
Tim Conway, so much talent
Harvey Korman, sweetheart
Thank God for Peter Marshall, Wally Cox, Charlie Weaver, Paul Lynde, Don Knotts, Louie Nye, and Tom Poston
My dear friends—my angels
George Gobel, Tony Randall, Phil Silvers—God bless those guys
Robert Goulet, talk about getting goose pimples
Mary Tyler Moore, God bless her
Shelley Fabares, thank God her jeans were tight
Very few shows on television are even worth watching
Thank God things worked out
Good God—Honk if you love Jesus
…Tell you about my wedding night
Heavenly Honeymoon
It's too much to describe
I was so dumb
I knew nothing of sex
Bobby was so wonderful
First trumpeter for Bing Crosby
Talk about thrills
I was in heaven, heaven on earth
Thank the Lord
…I believed in charity
Not to be a show off
My next project was a bazaar
This was a bazaar to end all bazaars
The church needed money—don't they always
Didn't cost the church a single penny
Raised $506, a tidy sum in those days
Those were the days
…Talk about a smartass
In show business since I'm three
A three-year old kid who sings like Sophie Tucker

Baby Rose Marie, the child wonder
Always working, thank God
Song and dance, vaudeville and nightclubs
A weekly radio show
Off Broadway, Broadway
Talk about a shock
Television (sitcoms and dramas—game shows)
Movies
Dinner theater engagements
After the curtain came down
I went home and prayed
I just stared into space and prayed quietly
I just prayed
...Life is funny—look at my life
Had a few laughs and tried to make the best of this mess
Everything that happens in life has been planned
What can I say—life is a three-legged chair
No rhyme or reason
Thank God for no rhyme or reason

From *Hold the Roses* by Rose Marie. University of Kentucky Press, 2003.

HIGH ON ARRIVAL

Everyone knew I was
Papa John's daughter.

Dad was fabulously
Rich and famous, the
Leader and songwriter
Of the Mamas & the Papas.

The limo would roll to a stop
In front of our condo.

We were special.
We were royalty.

We would climb in
Hoping to see our father.

He was never there.

One Day at a Time
Was everything.

Originally, in the pilot,
One Day at a Time
Was built around
My character.

Julie Cooper.

I had no idea
How significant
The role
Would be
In my life.

Dad ditched my mother
For a sixteen-year-old girl.

I was conceived
During a short
Reconciliation.

Dad was almost six foot six
And he dressed in handmade
Floor-length caftans.

He looked like
Jesus in tie-dye.

This alone was enough
To make a princess out of me.

Performing in front of
The studio audience,
I finally had
The attention
I'd always wanted.

Bonnie Franklin,
My mother on the show,
Assumed I was older.

Too old to be
Her daughter.

I looked up to Bonnie.
She could have been
The parental figure
That I so needed.

A precocious kid
With a desire
To act older.

I didn't feel
Like a kid.

I wore platforms
That made me
Six feet tall.

I wore tight jeans
And leather jackets.

I wore shades.

Clubbing on Sunset Strip.

Stealing drugs
From Dad
Became my
Not-so-secret
Habit.

Getting high.

Being a Philips
Meant getting high.

Valerie Bertinelli was
My younger sister
On TV.

We were only six months apart
In age, but she seemed like
A young child to me.

I was a lot taller than she was
And different in every way.

Val and I formed
A special bond,
In spite of our
Differences.

Dad was the great and terrible sun
Around which his children, wives,
Girlfriends, fellow musicians, and
Drug dealers orbited, drawn to his
Fierce, inspiring, damaging light.

Valerie was bubbly,
Clean, and eager.

I was the black sheep
They never stopped loving,
Hoping I'd come back
To the fold.

But, like the sisters
We played on TV,
We had a bond
That would
Always exist.

I was a thin,
Folded piece
Of paper
Pretending
To be
A person.

I used people
To get what
I wanted.

I tested people's
patience and tolerance.

My doctor
Prescribed Opana,
An opiate twice
As strong
As OxyContin

Val and I both went
To school on set.
Four hours per day
In twenty-minute
Increments.

Our differences,
Like our characters,
Would grow
More dramatic
Over the years
And pull us apart.

Feel no evil.

There's an upside
And a downside.

Feeling no evil
Helped me
Stay alive.

There are happy
Memories
Of the stable
Work and family
I found on
One Day at Time.

Of course—Schneider.
The comic relief.

Pat Harrington
As Schneider
Would tease me.

He'd call me
Q-Tip with eyes.

Drug use had taken
A toll on my appearance.

I was painfully thin
And my skin was terrible.

Skinny wasn't
Joke material
For Schneider
Anymore.

Oh, Schneider.
Where were you
When I needed you
For cheap laughs?

For all the lax parenting,
For all the hitchhiking
To school and empty
Refrigerators, for all the
Joint-rolling and
Coke-supplying,
I wanted to
Believe
I had a father
Who cared.

The happy memories of the stable
Work family I found on *One Day at a Time*.

The dichotomy.

I started to use
During the day.

I was a walking skeleton.
I was broken, half dead.
I felt soul sick.

What was it that made
My father so compelling?

People were so drawn to him,
Musicians, thinkers, women.

He was tall and cool.
Always fabulously dressed.

He drove fancy cars.
Threw outrageous parties.

His light was magnified for me.
I always wanted to be closer.

I was fired from
One Day at a Time.

I was using.

Val saw me
On the monitor
Nodding off,
Unable to keep
My eyes open.

I was blacklisted.
Word was out.
I was unreliable.
Nobody wanted
To hire me.

I watched Dad put some coke into
A spoon, pour distilled water into
A syringe, and squirt it into the spoon.

He used the plunger
To mix the powder
And water. He tore
The cotton off a Q-Tip
And dropped it into
The solution.

He pulled the liquid through
The cotton into the syringe.

I put my right arm out.
He tied me off.

Daddy's little girl.
All grown up.

The New Mamas & the Papas,
In reconstituted form,
Included my father and me.
In many ways, a dream come true.

I had blackouts during shows.

Dad and I got so high
People booed us and
Asked for their money back.

So much weirdness every day
That weirdness became everyday.

I was happy to be
Where I was.
With my Dad.
Doing drugs
Day and night.

Being a jet-setting junkie
Wasn't a big deal.

But I wasn't
All confidence.

Deeply into needles,
Heroin was burnt
On my soul.

I was using and living
Like a pig. Shooting.

Sleeping for days.
Shooting up for days.

Nobody grows up thinking,
I want to be a junkie
But in a weird way I did.

A father-daughter
Relationship that crossed
The boundaries of love
To break many taboos
As my father
Was wont to do.

When my father and I
Went through rehab together
The headline on the cover of *People*
Called us John & Mackenzie Phillips.

As if we were married.

All those years of free passes.
Freebasing. All those blind eyes.

Part of me still believed
I could get out of anything.

Busted at the airport.
Heroin possession.

The former child star.
The middle-aged lady.
A low low moment.

Incest is
An abuse
Of privilege,
An abuse
Of trust.

I desperately
Wanted to be
Close to him.
I needed him.

Your father
Is supposed to
Protect you
Not fuck you.

Sobriety was
My protection.
He was
Never going to
Touch me again.

I threw myself
Into rehabilitation.

Stripping down
To worthlessness.
Rebuilding ego.

Healing and growing.
Succumbing to

Powerlessness.

Reality is warped.
Shitloads of drugs
Will do that to you.

You can't
Believe the notes
Your sober self
Left your high self.

Self-destruction.
Rehabilitation.
Birth and death.
Love, drama, and pain.

I have demons,
Haunted parts
Of my life.

When Dad died
I was free.

After all those years
Waiting for my father.

I don't wait anymore.

From *High on Arrival* by Mackenzie Phillips. Gallery Books, 2009.

I AM NOT SPOCK

Mr. Spock has pointed ears
And arched eyebrows
And greenish skin
And wears his hair in bangs
And has a uniform with a blue shirt
And black pants
And boots
And he's on TV.

This man doesn't have any of those things.

That's not Mr. Spock.
He's standing here,
And he's not on TV.

I play a character called
Mr. Spock on the TV.
I have often been
Mistakenly referred to as
Dr. Spock—the well-known
Pediatrician.

I'll never really understand why
I was chosen to play Mr. Spock.

In a meta-physical sense
There seemed to be a sort of
Inevitability involved.

A successful mating of role and actor.
A man can cast a shadow not his own.

I am very much affected
By the clothes I wear.

Putting on a cape
Can make me feel.

An old work jacket,
Work boots, and an

Old dirty cap
Can make me feel.

Clothes affect me inwardly.
As does makeup.

Without Spock, who am I?

Had someone told me that
I was wonderful (they didn't)
I would have had to believe it.

If they had told me that
I was awful (mercifully, they didn't)
I would have been forced to believe *that*.

I was too curious.
I trusted my own taste.

Externals to me are very helpful.
Perhaps Spock had many births.

The supposedly *ahuman*, Spock. Outside the
Social mainstream—separate, unequal and alien.

He finds himself totally alienated
From both worlds. Trying to
Alienate himself, he reached
Pure alien status.

He recognizes this fact.
He enjoys it.

All of this was
Preparation for
The role of Spock.

Spock was a character
Whose time had come.

There is a popular notion
That actors are paid residuals
Each time a show is rerun.
This is only partly true.

We are paid for the first
Six runs or five reruns.

I don't keep the image
Of Spock alive.
I have done nothing
To further the life
Of Mr. Spock.
My concern
Is Leonard Nimoy.

We are resolved
To be logical.

Logical—that's *his* word,
Spock's word, and every-
Body knows it.

To this day, I sense
Vulcan speech patterns,
Vulcan social attitudes,
And even Vulcan patterns of
Logic and emotional suppression
In my behavior.

Look at the Spock character.
He knows what is appropriate.
He is always rational.

There seems to be a caring force,
Which enables him to be this way.

Of course, he did have
An earth mother.

He's here. Spock is here.
But he is he. He is not me.

I am not him.

With Spock and me,
It's a unique game of
"I'm O.K. We're O.K."

The Corsican brothers
Could exist in two places
At the same time.
Spock and I cannot.

We exist independently.
Spock is not my brother.

Do I or would I
Exist without him?

And without me
Who is he?

I am not Spock. But if I had to be
Someone else, I would be Spock.

I like him. I admire him. I respect him.

He stands for something.
Dignity and honesty.
And a lot more.

He's my best friend.
He's the only one
Who understands me.

Live Long and Prosper—L'Chaim!

From *I Am Not Spock*, by Leonard Nimoy. Buccaneer Books, 1975.

I AM SPOCK

You're Leonard Spock!

My son watches him on TV all the time!

The pointy-eared guy!

The devilish-looking alien, Spock.

A green-blooded
Pointy-eared alien
From outer space.

From *Star Trek*.

I'm not Spock.

But if I'm not, who is?

And if I'm not Spock
Then who am I?

Is Spock simply a "mask" I wear?

A good argument
Could be made
That I am Spock.

I am not Spock.

I'm an actor
Best known for playing
That character.

Space aliens were generally portrayed
As evil monsters bent on conquering Earth.

I felt very much an alien, an outsider, as a young boy.

The Enterprise had to have an alien
Crewmember, or she wouldn't fly.

I was branded as *The Man with the Pointed Ears.*
Every article about me in the press
Was laden with ear puns.

Headlines like, EARS TO LEONARD NIMOY.

The ears were something
Of a blessing and a curse.
They weren't painful
Just a little uncomfortable.

I suggested pointed sideburns
As a specifically Vulcan look.

Vulcans are galactic trendsetters.
Hardy souls distinguished by
A different skin color.
Those pointed sideburns.
Those damned pointed ears.

Something had to be done about the ears.
The effects house creating the ears
Wasn't right for the job. They were
Used to making big feet and hands for
Monster movies.

We had the proper skin tone
A yellowish-green, which
Looked far better on a
Black-and-white TV screen
Than red skin.

The yak-hair
(yes, yak hair)
Eyebrows were
Working, and
Even the haircut
Was working.

Spock's "look" was starting to gel.

Obviously extraterrestrial.
Interplanetary.

I am Spock.
Green-blooded
Patron saint of
Computer scientists.

Spock for President reads the bumper
Sticker on the car in front of me.

I feel a wonderful warmth
When I hear or read
A compliment aimed
At the Vulcan.

I'm filled with
Pride and I smile.

I'm not Spock.

I am not Spock.
I am merely a
Fictional character.

Half-human and half-alien.
Raised in a world where
Emotional displays were
In bad taste and firmly
Suppressed.

A very rich internal life.

This rational
Repressed side
Would
Of course
Overshadow
His emotional
Human side.

But...But?

Just how seriously
Could the viewing
Audience take a
Character with
Pointed ears?

I am aware of a certain
Public interest that exists.
Popularity does put one
In strange company.

The majority of Mr. Spock's fans were women.
It hadn't occurred to me that Mr. Spock was sexy...
That girls palpitate over the way one eyebrow
Goes up a fraction; that they squeal with
Passion when a little smile quirks his lip.

Erotic dream material for
Thousands and thousands of
Ladies around the world.

Fascinating.

Spock was sexy to female viewers
Precisely because he was smart.

Mr. Spock is Dreamy.
Spock is utterly Vulcan.
I am decidedly un-Vulcan

In preparing to play the character
I had already done some thinking
About Vulcan culture and customs
And had made a decision that the
Vulcans were a touch-oriented society,
As they were touch telepaths.

Based on that concept, the famous
Neck pinch was born—applied pressure
To the juncture of neck and shoulder.

More intriguing than the
Vulcan neck pinch was
The Vulcan mind-meld, joining
Consciousness—a very dangerous,
Risky thing.

I am not Spock.
I am Spock.
Both logical.
And accurate.

Half human.
Half Vulcan.

In full Vulcan regalia, I am Spock.

Have you lost your small
Glass gaming spheres?
You are not Spock.

Vulcan logic has had
A tempering effect on my
Emotional human personality.

I am a Vulcan!
I am in control
Of my emotions!

Spock, I don't harbor any feelings of
Jealousy or competition toward you.
After all, I am you. And you're me.
You sprang from who I am.

A bright message of hope in the form of *Star Trek.*

We will survive the atomic age.
We will contact other intelligent life on other planets.
They'll be our friends, not our enemies.
Together, we'll work for the common good.

I don't hate Spock or *Star Trek.*
It wasn't my idea to kill the character.

Star Trek and Spock
Are dear to my heart.

Emotion versus logic.
Love versus mathematics.
Grief versus pi-r-squared.

Never again the raised eyebrow.
Never again the mind-meld,
The neck pinch, or the Vulcan
Salute and blessing.

Live long and prosper, Spock.
Live long and prosper.

Just another
One of thousands
Of death scenes.

I was experienced.
I'd died before.
On TV.

From *I Am Spock* by Leonard Nimoy. Hyperion Books, 1995.

YOU CAN'T MAKE THIS UP

What I try to do on TV is strike the right tone, match the words to the action without necessarily using a lot of verbs.

On radio, verbs are very important. On television, viewers absorb action with their own eyes and the verbs are being

played visually in their brains. Often, ellipses can suffice. No superfluous adjectives needed. On television less is more.

Cadence. Delivery. The art of inflection. A wonderful way with words, supplemented by a phenomenal memory, the

play-by-play announcer has to speak in quick bites. In a manner of speaking, authority, warmth, knowledge,

creativity, and, most important of all, the rhythm. Style, a twinkle in the voice. Pronounce every name correctly. Show

everyone how smart you are. Show that you know every player's middle name. Tell the truth. Tell the story. Tell

the viewer what you know. Something to avoid—the phrase, "This puts everything into perspective." Just

for the record, this is Al Michaels, a self-promoting and incessantly self-aggrandizing, self-anointed wunderkind.

This is Al Michaels, always genuinely modest. Remarkably humble and rarely comfortable with praise. Just happy to

be here, friend, in a manner of speaking. Because the games. Because sports. Because ESPN. Now, here we are at the

1980 Winter Olympics. Lake Placid, New York. The USA-USSR game. A word pops into my head—miraculous. A split second

later, it gets morphed into a question and answer. My voice. I said, "Do you believe in miracles. Yes!" Six words. Crowd

noise. To this day, I can still hear that sound in my mind's ear, this booming voice—that unmistakable bellowing voice. I said,

"Do you believe in miracles. Yes!" My voice, in disbelief, heading
into a much higher octave. Immediately before I said, "Do you

believe in miracles," I said, "Morrow, up ahead to Silk, five
seconds left in the game..." A perfect description. I had been

concentrating on getting the play-by-play perfect. I let the
pictures tell the story. Brief. Concise. I let the scene play

out. Adding anything more would be redundant. One of
those *one-for-the-ages* magical performances. What I live for.

Since I was six years old, I wanted to be a sports broadcaster.
I dreamed of announcing Major League Baseball, the NFL

on TV. My dreams were as big as they could be—to make it in
broadcasting. You don't want to underplay what's exhilarating.

But you don't want to be over-the-top. I took my broadcasting
seriously. A broadcaster, excited to talk about all sports, always

remembering how lucky I've been. Even after all these years,
inevitably, someone in the stands will yell out, "Hey, Al. Do you

believe in miracles?" I always say, "Yes." Decades later people
come up to me on the street and say, "Do you believe in miracles?"

I often get asked to record messages for answering machines. They
ask, "Al, can you please say, 'Do you believe Bob is away from

his desk right now? Yes!!!'" Been there, done that. And I have
this crazy, unscripted drama known as sports to thank for it all.

Still roaming the earth. Still another game to come. Still perfecting
how to use my voice as an instrument. Still working, play by play.

Here we are thirty-plus years later and Lake Placid still resonates.
I said, "Do you believe in miracles." Then I paused and said, "Yes!"

From *You Can't Make This Up* by Al Michaels. William Morrow, 2014.

LOVELOSSANDWHATWEATE

asafortysomething
womanonTV
Iamarapidly
depreciatingasset

asagirl
Imadeagame
ofstompingandsquishing
fallenkumquats
dozensofdustykumquats
asIwalkedtoschool

— o —

bait
awormtoafish
afishtoabear
amangotoanIndiangirl

wetdollopsofrice
gingeranddriedgreenmango
fatandspices
onionandchutneys
goldenchutney
bathedinjustenoughheat
garnishedwithadollopofrelish

— o —

Ikissedtwoboys
inoneafternoon
duringafieldtrip
toanamusementpark

anamuse-bouche
kissingkissing
chefkiss

— o —

Ihadadramofsuccess
asamodel
walkingtherunway
lingeriemodeling

Ilivedtheclichésthatcomewithmodeling
partyingonyachts
wearingonlymybikinibottom

ifIknewsomeonewaswatching
Imightturnsomyscarwasvisible
myscarbecameadornment
likeastringofpearls

— o —

everyonewantstoknowwhatamodeleats

sourhomemadeplainyogurt
murkybeefbroth
hugesalads
curriesandsoupylentils
ladledoverrice

aHinduBrahminlacto-vegetariandiet

asteadydietofchips
(somecrunchysomesoggy)
tartspicysalsas
coolingdollops
ofsourcream
garbanzobean
greenbean
softbutterywhitebean
seanbean
drinkingpinotnoir
champagnewhiskey
LedZeppelinandspicyfood
Coca-Cola
tacosdumplingsbarbeque
rockcandy
cranberrygreenteadrano
tohelpcleanse
mydigestivepipes

afterallthe
gluttonous

— o —

SalmanRushdie
wantedtoknow
thecolorof
mypeach

daringtoeatapeach

— o —

grandliterarydinners
namedrop
literaryrockstars
SusanSontag
PeterCarey
DonDeLillo
PaulAuster
andhissecondwife
SiriHustvedt

— o —

eatingwasameansofbeautification
themoreyouconsumed
themorelikelyyoud
reachavoluptuousness

— o —

ontheshow
judgestable
adifficultdish
joltingmypalate

quickfire
bitebitebite
taste-of-this
taste-of-that
pause
scrunchingupmyfacethewholetime

inscrutablefacialexpression
spewavaguecomment
givenothingaway
andrepeat

inthemidstofculinaryheavyweights
nothingmorethanaprettyface

— o —

menontvhaveuniforms
boxysuits
blackblueorgray

Iamtheonewhohasto
looklikeaglorified
weathergirl
formfittingdressandall

theconstantstruggle
thatpervadesmylife
howdoIlookgood
andstillbegoodatmyjob
howdoIexperience
enoughfoodsoIknow
whatIamtalkingaboutontv
andstilllookgood
whiletalkingaboutit

— o —

Icouldnoteat
fromdepression
andwassothin

meremonthslater
aftermydivorce
andanotherseason
ofTopChef
Iballoonedup
twodresssizes

everywomanhasarecordofherbody
aclosetfullofjeansandbrasofvarioussizes

albumsfullofphotographs
photographsrevealing
revealingweightgainandloss

aphotographisnotanopinion

— o —

Ialwayscomehungry
bringing
thefullaudienceofmyappetite

mystomach
arestaurantdumpster
devastatedbymyfullness

theprizeofwinning
wasnolonger
aflatstomach

managemyjobandmyappearance

gaintwentypounds
acinchandapleasure
everygroceryrunatreasure
somesmallmeasure
ofjoy

— o —

whenasnackcombined
saltinesstartnesssweetnessandspiciness
inthatmagicalmouth-smackingproportion
thenthatsnackhadchaatpati

— o —

apalatemustbetrained
stimulatedcultivatedbuffered
dicedmincedslicedchoppedcarved
squeezedfolded
spoonedladledpouredforked
choppedgingerandhotgreenchilies
simplifiedthespicesmostly

noodlesincoconutmilk
starchy-stickyalittleicky
softbananalumps
mashedintocardamom-infusedsweetcoldmilk

eatingontheshow
turnedmeon
felttomeliketheprom
Ineverhad

— o —

totrulyhavea
womanlyfigure
youhavetoeat
tobevoluptuously
fulloffood
myboobs
bothnipplesblazing
milkshakes
themellowbuzz
likethetipsinessofchampagne
acelebrationoffood

— o —

vanitykickedin
vanityispowerful
vanityhadgovernedmyeatinghabits
vanitykeptmefromgivingintofriedchicken

apicnicabrunchalunchadinnerparty

thisweightgain
wasunlikemypastfluctuations.
Ifeltliberatedfromtheworriesaboutmyfigure
liberatedfromtheworriesaboutmyfigure

— o —

asapracticalmatter
Ihavecometoaccept
weightgainaspartofmy
TopChef

pactwiththedevil
(toputitmildly)

eating
themostintimateact
eatingthings
eatingtoomuchcheese
eatingmeat
eatingalot
eatingwell
eatinghotelroomservice
eatingafalafel
eatingachaatburger
eatingcoqauvinanddrinkingpinotnoir
eatingintinyportions
eatingfugues
eatingthatlusciousegg
eatingfortwo
eatingmyplacenta

afteralifetime
infrontofthecamera
myfigureasourceofstatus

myfortiethbirthday
wouldusherinafundamentalshift
inthetrajectoryofmybreastsarmsandthighs

Ilikedmybodyasitrounded
sexyvoluptuousinashesabrickhouseway
hotandhotterandhottest

From *Love, Loss, and What We Ate* by Padma Lakshmi. Ecco/HapererCollins, 2016.

MY LIFE AS A 10-YEAR-OLD BOY

1. What if I told you I was Bart Simpson?
2. I am a professional ten-year-old boy on TV.
3. Although I own my voice, I don't own Bart's voice.
4. I don't ad-lib a whole lot for Bart—I stick to the script.
5. My voice in a talking Bart doll (pull string): Bart says, Eat my shorts. Bart says, No way, man! Bart says, Don't have a cow! Bart says, Ay caramba! Bart says, Sacre bleu!
6. I know the difference between a cartoon and reality.
7. I get a lot of, Do Bart! Do Bart! Do Bart!
8. Understanding the Bart in me—dealing with the Bart in me—this is not black and white.
9. The way I see it, I was destined to be Bart.
10. I'm Nancy Cartwright. Who the hell are you?!

1. I'm Bart Simpson. Who the hell are you?!
2. Bart on his skateboard in the opening credits.
3. Bart, sitting on the couch watching Krusty on TV.
4. Even after studying hard, Bart still fails his history test.
5. Bart is in the fourth grade—forever.
6. There is an emotional aspect to Bart.
7. Bugs Bunny and Mickey Mouse and Bart Simpson.
8. Bart's not such a bad role model.
9. Do the Bartman. Do the Bartman. Do the Bartman!
10. From the mouth of Bart herself, God Bless the Child.

From *My Life as a 10-Year-Old Boy* by Nancy Cartwright. Hyperion, 2000.

PRICELESS MEMORIES

On TV
For decades
Daytime
Game show profits
Helped to fund
The networks'
More expensive
Primetime
Programming
Jeopardy!
What's My Line?
To Tell the Truth
Wheel of Fortune
I had thirty-five
Great years on
The Price is Right
You never knew
Who would win
You can be
A policeman
A doctor
A writer
A cabdriver
You identify
With the prices
Oh, that's a good bid
Or that's not enough
Whatever the case may be
A ridiculous bid
Could be
Just as much fun
As an accurate bid
We also had beautiful models
Barker's Beauties
Beautiful women who
Displayed the prizes
Demonstrated merchandize
Provided ample grace
And beauty
We had a solid

Structure and format
Three games
The wheel
Three more games
The second wheel
And the showcase
At the end of the show
We were
The first
Game show
To succeed
As an hour-long show
More time to have fun
With the contestants
And the audience
People love to win prizes
In 1987
I went on vacation
And let my hair go gray
Everyone agreed
That it looked better
Than tinted or dyed
It was a little
Revolutionary
At the time
I do not think
There was another
Gray-haired
Game show
Host on air
TV Guide called
The Price is Right
The number one
Game show
Of all time
Very popular
One of the great parts
Of my job as host
Was to bring out
Humor in people
Someone once said
That I make my living
Making other people
Funny

I played straight man
For the contestant
I was always Bob Barker
Come on down
Just three words
Come on down
To Contestants' Row
Come on down
Of course
The all-time
On-air
Mishap
Was the lady
In the tube top
Jumping
Up and down
And her breasts
Popped out
Come on down
People think
The show is simple
And relatively easy
To produce
It is a fast-moving show
Elaborate set pieces
Difficult for
The cameramen
A challenge for
The stagehands
Constantly shuttling
Props
Games
Prizes
Around the set
Choosing contestants
Like casting a play or movie
Some people have this wonderful thing
Everybody loves them
Right away
In an effort
To make
A better world
For animals
The show

Stopped
Giving away
Fur or leather products
The fur flap
My animal rights activism
My beliefs
My vegetarianism
We stopped giving away
Aquariums and fishing equipment
Media attention focused on
The animal rights movement
I talked about my pets
And for years
I ended the show with
Help control
The pet population
Have your pets
Spayed or neutered

From *Priceless Memories* by Bob Barker. Center Street, 2009.

RANDOM ACTS OF BADNESS

— two villanelles —

Act I.

I loved being Danny Partridge and I still love it.
I was the star of the show. I always had the most lines.
I was a kid actor, flame-haired (and mouthy).

The Partridge Family were the original Milli Vanilli.
I couldn't fake the bass and make it look realistic.
I loved being Danny Partridge and I still love it.

Some people might have been embarrassed. Not I.
Most people make asses of themselves on TV.
I was a kid actor, flame-haired (and mouthy).

The star of a number one TV show, I was never an actor.
I never claimed to be. I was a showoff. There's a difference.
I loved being Danny Partridge and I still love it.

The Partridge Family ended without any fanfare.
I was fourteen. I was a hit. I was canceled. I was shit.
I was a kid actor, flame-haired (and mouthy).

I waited for what was next. I wondered if anybody cared.
Being a child star is a party. Being an ex-child star sucks.
I loved being Danny Partridge and I still love it.
I was a kid actor, flame-haired (and mouthy).

Act II.

I was the guy from *The Partridge Family.*
I was the boy wonder on the set, a genius IQ.
I wasn't a joke. I wasn't a loser.

I would go to bed almost every night buzzed.
I would wake up at ten, have a couple drinks.
I was the guy from *The Partridge Family.*

I was not taking drugs to get high but in
An attempt to kill Danny Partridge.
I wasn't a joke. I wasn't a loser.

I was cross-addicted. Drug addict. Sex addict.
The two big NO-NOs of rehab were sex and drugs.
I was the guy from *The Partridge Family.*

I proved author F. Scott Fitzgerald wrong.
There were second acts in American lives.
I wasn't a joke. I wasn't a loser.

Disney and NBC apparently want me on TV,
Child star and former poster boy of bad behavior.
I was the guy from *The Partridge Family.*
I wasn't a joke. I wasn't a loser.

From *Random Acts of Badness* by Danny Bonaduce. Hyperion, 2001.

BOSSYPANTS

So...

You ended up on TV
Because Lorne Michaels
Likes to promote
From within.

Some people arrive
At the show sane
And the show
Turns them crazy.

You just glided in
On a dog sled
With your pageant sash
And Tina Fey glasses.

Why not write about
What it's like to work
At *SNL*? A book about
The making of a woman.

Yes, and. Improvisation.
Improv. In improv there are
No mistakes. YES, AND.
Comedy is about confidence.

You could piece
Something together
With Lorne Michaels
As a symbol for God.

Funny and controlling
At the same time. A boss
And amazingly funny.
A natural bossypants.

Do you know anyone
Personally that you
Would describe as a
Bossypants?

Being the boss almost never
Involves marching around,
Waving your arms, chanting,
I am the boss! I am the boss!

You're the boss. You're in charge.
You're under forty. You're lucky.
Pretend you are not the boss,
When you're the boss.

You're a diehard foodie,
Gastronomically adventurous.
You actually eat food. You've been
Eating like a hog lately.

Eating pizza. Eating cashews.
Onion rings. Count Chocula. Cold Roy
Rogers fries. Peel-and-eat-shrimp.
Pickled eggs. A Subway Sandwich.

Wawa Italian hoagie.
A cheesesteak with
Provolone cheese.
Milk shake. Ten Eggs.

Eat food. Lean hard into the food.
Desserts. Ice cream. Cake. Pies.
Miniature lemon meringue pies.
Rows and rows of pastries.

Get a Whopper Jr. at
Burger King.
Then go to McDonald's
To get the fries.

Your heart could not stop
Eating itself. Eating Santa's face.
Sweet potato fries. Homemade
Nachos. Constantly eating.

You're recognized by the guy
Who refills the soft-serve machine
By the pool but not for being
On TV, just for lingering.

Like eating an apple and smoking
A cigarette at the same time,
Writing is a solitary experience.
Not unlike a dog, you have options.

Panning for gold.
Jokes. Golden nuggets
Shit nuggets. Knowing
The difference.

Jerry Lewis says,
Women aren't funny.
You don't fucking care.
It's irrelevant.

Flatulence jokes first.
Feminist consciousness-
Raising second. Whatever's
The funniest. At the moment.

Improv as metaphor for virtue.
Improv for a spiritual allegory.
God had a sense of humor. He's
A fan of *Saturday Night Live*.

Do you think it's good
That you're angry? Do
You think you're more
Important than everybody?

Your energy is better used
Doing your work. Outpacing
People. Old improv saying,
Do it now. Do it too. Do it again.

Oprah Winfrey is suggesting you
May have overextended yourself.
If you're so mad you could
Just cry, then cry. YES, AND...

You feel like Beyoncé.
You look weird. You
Look tired. You look
Like a cadaver. Boo.

You look as good as you can.
You look like you have no lips.
You look like a crazy asshole.
You look ridiculous.

If you don't have a good body,
You'd better starve the body
You have down to a neutral
Shape. Very very skinny.

Then bolt on some breast
Implants. Replace your teeth.
Dye your skin orange. Inject
Your lips, sew on some hair.

You were either blessed with
A beautiful body or not. If
You were not, just chill
Out and learn a trade.

It's good that you're angry
It's *good* that you're angry.
Start with a YES and see
Where it takes you.

In real life you're not
Always going to agree
With everything everyone
Says. Yes, and...

Leave people alone
About their weight.
Don't ever get punched
In the face. Elementary.

Glasses made you awesome.
A commonplace librarian
Fetish embraced. Glasses!
An Oprah "Aha Moment."

Do your thing and don't care
If they like it. Or not. A woman
Who keeps talking. Assert that
You are *not* a butterface.

The future is a gender-blind
Meritocracy of whoever
Is really the funniest.
Today is about dreams!

YES, AND...

From *Bossypants* by Tina Fey. Reagan Arthur Books, 2011.

"Everyone likes to watch kids dancing on TV."
— Dick Clark

ROCK, ROLL & REMEMBER

I lived the image
Expected of me
On TV.

Live from Philadelphia.
American Bandstand.
A new teen-age paradise.

A big promotion
Plugged the show.
An invitation for kids.

A thousand kids showed up
That first afternoon. Could only get
Two hundred at a time in the studio.

Come to Bandstand,
Teen-agers. Come to
Dance on Bandstand.

The Alligator. The Bop. The Boston Monkey.
The Bristol Stomp. The Bunny Hop.
The Cool Jerk. The Dicky Doo. The Duck.

Dancing was the result
Of putting together
The kids and the music.

Make kids dancing
The visual portion
Of the program.

Bandstand determined
The dance steps
Of teenage America.

The Fly. The Frug. The Harlem Shuffle.
The Hitchhike. The Hully Gully.
The Jitterbug. Limbo. The Lindy.

Tune in between 3:30 and 5:00 to
Pick up new steps. Bandstand
Was on every afternoon.

One star after another
Coming out to lip-sync
His or her latest hit.

Bobby Darrin. Bobby Helms.
Bobby Rydell. Bobby Sheehan.
Bobby Soxx. Bobby Vee.

The Chantels. The Diamonds.
Dicky Doo and the Don'ts.
The Dubs. The Four Preps.

Ames Brothers. Everly Brothers.
Isley Brothers. The Osmonds.
Jerry Lee Lewis. Carl Perkins.

Peggy Lee. Connie Francis.
Patti Page. Annette Funicello
And Frankie Avalon.

Usually some kind
Of low-budget
Production number.

At the Hop. Book of Love.
Get a Job. La De Dah. Splish
Splash. Who's Sorry Now?

A Spotlight Dance—a slow
Dance—the cameras got close
On one couple dancing.

Slow dancing was the
Art of getting sexually
Aroused with no payoff.

Elvis and Ricky Nelson,
Ricky Nelson and Elvis Presley,
Two stars who never did the show.

Call Bobby or Frankie and
They'd hop in their cars and be
At the studio within 15 minutes.

Bobby and Connie,
They'd sign autographs.
They loved the star treatment.

Fabian was a shy kid.
Fats Domino was terrified
Of appearing on TV.

Paul Anka was the first super-
Star I ever met who wrote
And performed his own songs.

Bobby Darin had a bad heart. Bobby
Had a fear he wasn't going to grow old,
That he wouldn't live long.

Chubby was looking for his big break.
Chubby had no original material.
Chubby went to number one.

A gang of kid dancers
And a current rock star
Gallivanting around.

Playing the best sounds
In town, platters spinning
On TV.

The Loco-Motion. The Madison.
The Mashed Potato. The Peppermint Twist.
The Pony. The Popeye. The Shag.

The Shake. The Stroll. The Swim.
The Twist. The Walk. The Watusi.
The Wiggle. The Wiggle Wobble.

Bandstand will go on forever.
Not bad for a guy with a
Short attention span.

The secret to my success?
My ego is well-developed.
I'm a reasonably smart fellow.

Let me finish with a toast.
You've gotta live for today.
You can't live in the past.

Good times won't come 'round again.
So here's to you...my friend...
We shared some happy days!

From *Rock, Roll & Remember* by Dick Clark. Thomas Y. Crowell & Co., 1976.

SUNDAY NIGHTS AT SEVEN

I am not a happy comedian—I am a frustrated violinist.

Cracking wise with my fellow vaudeville troupers on stage.
Forty million listeners—on radio.
A long and successful sojourn on TV.

— o —

In vaudeville a great act could last a lifetime.
Some vaudeville acts didn't change a jot
Or a tittle in fifty years.

Smith & Dale, Fred Allen, W.C. Fields.

Radio longevity was briefer.
You could still survive
If you kept your program fresh.

But television!
To survive
Even five years
Is damn near
Impossible.

— o —

I'm told that when I was three years old, I liked to get a smile out of people by
Reciting poems and singing nursery rhymes.

Life in the Benny household was a barrel of laughs.
I was learning to get laughs by playing my fiddle
In funny ways and with gestures.

He don't practice
Mama said.
Without practicing
He'll be a nothing.
We didn't give you
Music lessons
So you should

Make a disgrace
Of yourself.

When I got to puberty, I became very interested in girls
And very much enjoyed what we then called "spooning."

At seventeen I was playing
In the pit orchestra
At one of two vaudeville
Theaters in Waukegan
Making $7.50 a week.

Learning show business
Through osmosis.

One week
The Marx Brothers
Came to town.

One of the outstanding
Rip-and-tear farcical
Acts in vaudeville.

Their mother
Ran the act.

She was impressed
By my playing and sight reading
And offered me $15 a week
Plus transportation and room and board
To travel with her young sons.

My parents turned it down flat.

If I had gone on the road
I might have become
So successful as a pit musician
Then I never would have
Become a comedian.

The years went by
And I was playing the best
Theaters and getting a
Good salary

Poor mama. She didn't live long.
I was a bitter disappointment—a cheap
Fiddle act in vaudeville and she never
Came to see me because she thought
Show business was immoral.

I was a headliner
In a way
Playing the next
To closing spot.

But I was not a star.

I did not become a star
Until I went on the radio.

— o —

So many sound cues
Slams of doors and
Opening of doors and
Creaking of doors.

New techniques in
Communicating comedy
Situations.

Building moments
And scenes
Just for the *ear.*

Footsteps here. Footsteps there.

How much we got out of
Footsteps and door slams
In those golden days of radio!

Listeners wanted stingy jokes
So I tried rationing them.
One stingy joke a program.

In my opinion
(which I highly value)
The finest joke I ever did
On radio was this one:

Walking home at night.
Sound effects of my footsteps.
Then somebody else's footsteps—behind me.
Holdup man shoves a gun in my ribs.

Your money or your life.
Your money or your life.
Your money—Stop nagging.
I'M THINKING IT OVER.

— o —

The switch to TV was imminent.

I remember the radio years with nostalgia.

Funny came naturally on radio.
Television was a different medium
And funny was harder work.

A weekly TV show took up so much more
Energy and time than radio—longer to
Write, longer to rehearse, longer to perform.

One damn funny TV show.
How the audience laughed.

A comedian is not necessarily someone who cracks jokes or
Makes funny expressions and does wild pieces of business.
Sometimes he or she is a subtle interpreter of lines and situations.

Pauses worked just as well visually.

Because the other actors were
Overplaying their parts
My slow, flat delivery sounded
Funny in contrast.

I was a master of *my* kind of timing.
I have a slowly paced delivery.

Television is wonderful
Entertainment.
But I miss radio.

I always thought radio was my métier.

Quite frankly
When I look at the old TV shows
And listen to the old Radio shows,
Radio holds up better,
Seems less dated.

People put on the television,
Watch it absentmindedly.

Jessel said,
Television is like having
Seven brothers-in-law
Living in your house.

From *Sunday Nights at Seven* by Jack Benny and his daughter Joan. Warner Brothers Books, 1990.

"He was just as he appeared on TV, a true gentleman."

THE ANSWER IS...

Who is...GEORGE ALEXANDER TREBEK?

Who is Alex Trebek?
How bright is he?
What is he like?

> I'm no different from many other people.
> I have never seen myself as anything special.
> I especially do not feel comfortable writing about myself.

What do you expect the benefits of a book will be for you?

> It's an aperçu of Alex Trebek, human being. A bit of a potpourri.
> A series of quick look-ins. Just hitting the highlights.

- o -

No matter what question they ask, if I provide
The same answer I will always get a laugh.

> I drink. What do you do when you're not working?
> I drink. What do you do to keep in shape?
> I drink. How do you prepare for the show?

...I wasn't a drinker.
I drink low-fat milk and
Chardonnay—but not together.
Got milk?

- o -

What is ... A MUSTACHE?

They're asking me about my mustache.
How do you feel about the mustache?

> I like the mustache. Very strongly.

I was the first game show
Host since Groucho Marx
To be on air with a mustache.

I was without a mustache from 2001 until 2014.
We put the vote to fans on whether I should keep it.
They voted I should shave it off again.

Look at all the tragedy and calamity going on in the world.
And they're asking me about my mustache. I grew it back.
They left me with my mustache.

- o -

Real hair or hairpiece?
How many feet are in a mile?
Where did Fibber McGee & Molly live?

Revelations? An end-of-life reconciliation
Or settling of old scores? Things like that?
Sometimes our values are a little off.

Hey, you didn't phrase that in the form of a question!
At the opening of *Jeopardy!* I'm introduced as "the host"
Rather than "the star." I insisted on that when I took the job in 1984.

It's easy to get in a rut.
There are only so many ways of saying
"Correct" or "That's right."

Should you not be concerned that by revealing stuff from your past you
Might lose some of the goodwill that has been coming your way? Is this just
An end-of-life reconciliation or settling of old scores?

> I had a good head of hair—a sort of pompadour
> With a ducktail in the back. A gentle voice.
>
> I'd often quiz my dad.
> What's to become of me?
> Am I just going to live from
> One game show to another?

Reach for the Top. Strategy. Pick and Choose. The Wizard of Odds. High Rollers. Double Dare. Pitfall. The $128,000 Question. Battlestars. Malcolm. Starcade. Classic Concentration. To Tell the Truth. Jeopardy!

Jeopardy! What a lovely show.
Giving the contestants the answers.
I enjoyed the work, and I was good at it.

- o -

Have you ever thought about retiring?

Do you know something, I don't?

If you have some sense of perspective
You are not likely to get too high or too low.

I'm a private person.
Like most people,
I want to be liked.

If manners prevent us from speaking the truth,
We will be without manners. I will say no more.

- o –

On the air.

The host of a television quiz show.

A good quiz show host.

Thank you very much.
It doesn't matter if you're wearing pants.

There are a lot of people who don't watch television.
You never want to inject too much of yourself into the show.

What's in it for you?
What's your favorite color?
How would you do as a contestant?
Which famous people would you have liked to see on the show?
What's your favorite book?

What are your favorite *Jeopardy!* categories?
What's the favorite place you traveled to with the show?
Is there any place still on your bucket list?
If you weren't hosting *Jeopardy!*, what would you be doing?

What's happening here?

What is a touchdown? What is an option play? What is fourth down? What is a fair catch? Who are the purple people eaters? Who are the Dallas Cowboys? What is holding? What is too many men on the field? What is a false start? What are offsetting penalties? Who do you think should replace you?

What's going on?
What the hell's going on?

What's the prognosis? What's important?

We're out to have a good time, eh?

Wait for the shit to hit the fan. Then we act.
We do not act beforehand.

That has always disappointed me
About the United States.

- o –

When I was younger, I had a great memory,
I didn't forget anything. Now my memory is fading.

Who's about to turn 80?

I'm in the same boat as Mark Twain, who in his seventies
Said he remembered only the things that never happened.

My powers of recall have slowed.
If that occurs here, tough shit.

Holy shit! (Alex Trebek Swears) Oh shit.

Diagnosed with stage IV pancreatic cancer.

Well, that changed everything, didn't it?

Fuck shit! Fuck shit! Fuck shit! Fuck shit! Fuck shit!
Cancer, chemotherapy and my age have taken a toll.

The answer is CURSING.

I was just fucking with you. You son of a bitch.

What's your job?

I know there will come a time when I can no longer do my job
as host—do it as well as the job demands, as well as I demand.

I'm glad I studied philosophy. Am I a believer?
I believe in the power of positivity.

I believe in the will to live. I believe in optimism. I believe in hope. I believe that's something you have to earn. I love acquiring knowledge, even useless knowledge. I'm curious about everything, even things that don't interest me. There's a thrill connected to curiosity. Because curiosity leads to discovery. And there's a thrill that comes with discovery. Jeez, how about that?!

What is retirement?

I wish I could stop and smell the roses.

What is the will to survive?

My dad didn't go to church. Mom did.
I went to mass every Sunday.
But do I pray to a specific god?

- o -

Do I anticipate a particular version of the Afterlife?
No, I do not. For all I know I'll wind up coming back as a knitter.

- o -

Merv Griffin wrote the *Jeopardy!* theme song. It's called "Think."
Merv originally wrote it as a lullaby for his son entitled "A Time for Tony."

Do you ever get tired of hearing it?

What do you think?

Shortly before his death, Merv admitted that the little *Jeopardy!* Think music earned him close to $80 million.

What do you know?

One contestant specialized in dream interpretation.
I'm always being chased in a recurring dream of mine.

What are your favorite *Jeopardy!* categories?

- o -

It's over. The game is over.

Am I bearing it well, or am I a coward?
Okay, how do I solve this?

The answer is...
The answer is...LIFE.

The winner is Alex Trebek.

Thank you very much. Goodbye.

From *The Answer Is...* by Alex Trebek. Simon & Schuster, 2020.

THE LEGS ARE THE LAST TO GO

Television's first black bitch
    on the TV series *Dynasty*
    submerged in the pageantry
    of big hair and bigger shoulders

I loved every minute of it

I felt beautiful and special from the start
    this little girl from Harlem
        I can sing
            I can dance

High cheekbones
    tall
    slim figure
    and the sincere innocence
    of the little lady
    I actually was
    trained to be
        a white-glove-wearing girl

Prim and proper in
    patent-leather shoes and
    a sky-blue smock dress
        or in a black and white
        school-girl dress with
        a Peter Pan collar

A girl who became a singing star
    in nightclubs and on television
    wearing pearls
        colorful clothes
        like a girl in a sparkly fantasy
            if you have sparkle on the sweater
            why not on the belt and skirt too

I was always on time
    always prepared
    and always *always*
    coiffed and dressed

My mother took me shopping
at Best & Company
for versions of the clothes
showing on the runways

I looked at myself in the mirror
Miss Smarty Pants
a slim young girl
counting on the legs

Cheekbones beyond fabulous

Light-skinned
passing the "paper-bag" test
meaning no darker in skin color
than a paper bag

Truman Capote and Harold Arlen
cast me as the ingenue in
House of Flowers

I had an innate ladylike quality
I was all about style and class
I oiled my legs
so they wouldn't look ashy

Make me up Asian
for *Flower Drum Song*

I had a reputation
of being fresh
not difficult
just strong-willed
I was a feisty little lady
I wasn't about small
I was always about big
I grew up on MGM musicals
that were as much about spectacle
as melody

Richard Rodgers
wrote a musical
for me called

        No Strings
                the first interracial romance
                Broadway had ever seen

It meant the world to depict
        a black woman with
        some sophistication

The networks summoned
        and I became NBC's *Julia*
                the first sitcom about
                a black character

A little equanimity
        can go a long way
                if you let every slur
                pull you off mark
                you are wasting your energy
                        you need to move forward

I don't think things are black and white
        excuse the pun
                I'm into shades of gray
                        as long as they aren't in my hair

At home
        I had a smart husband
                a kind man who loved to read
                        Mr. Diahann Carroll

I enjoyed being a wife
        at least for a while

I was nine months pregnant
        The process of
                childbirth
                        gestation
                                painful delivery
                                        bouncing baby

Not the product of my loins
        but rather my angst

Suddenly the nice

fun guy
turned into
a raging bully

I told him our marriage
never made sense
in the first place
filed papers for divorce
the next day in Reno

I was flat on my ass
I knew that I'd eventually
land on my feet

I never took any of the glamour for granted
a big fat blessing

My happy *Dynasty* period
my worries about
my career were at bay
I was having a big moment
the gift of *Dynasty*

When you live a life in which
racial prejudice is a daily experience
you carry with you a mental first-aid kit
to fix any situation
to avoid further
infection of your soul

Some people come of age
as teenagers
I came of age
as a senior citizen

A lovely thing
that comes as you age—forgiveness
and perhaps a relaxing of standards
just enough to give yourself
and others a break

No career is guaranteed
especially for an
African-American

woman in showbiz

I'm a performer
who still enjoys make-believe

Even though the tummy isn't
as taut as it used to be
the legs are still shapely and slender
they really are the last things to go
you know

From *The Legs are the Last to Go* by Diahann Carroll. Amistad, 2008.

What's it like, being the biggest
fucking idiot on TV?
I thought I was hot shit.
This dichotomy
bothered me.

BEHIND THE BELL

— tanka —

Samuel "Screech" Powers,
the stereotypical
nerdy-nerd, with the
white-tape-wound-around glasses,
the high-waters with white socks.

Saved by the Bell,
fresh-faced T & A on
TV for kids first
thing in the morning.
All the applause and laughs and

hoots and jeers were real.
I scored my share of coo-
chie backstage but it wasn't
easy. Screech received the
most fan mail…from fellow nerds.

This conflict between
the societal concept
of nerdiness and
the stock television por-
trayal of nerdiness is

what made Screech real.
Screech was the underdog. Screech
was a warm-hearted
goofball. I saw Screech as an
annoying nerd Everyman.

From *Behind the Bell* by Dustin Diamond. Transit Publishing, 2009.

ARE YOU ANYBODY?

Hey there's that guy on TV! Are you anybody?

Are you Mr. Salomone from the Plaza Hotel in *Eloise*?

It is not uncommon for people to think I'm Dr. Phil
  and thank me for all the good I'm doing.
It is not uncommon for people to think I'm Larry David
  and thank me for all the good I'm doing.

People think I'm the man on the subway in *Ghost*.

Are you anybody? The Mayor of Whoville? Long pause. No.

My first thought in the morning is, Oh, no.

Are you okay? Are you anybody?
  Are you going to be all right?

Here I am removing the spell...

Think you're the best. Think you're astonishing.
Think you're one of the finest actors out there.
Think you're Hank Kingsley. Hey now!

My dragonfly mind, flitting from subject to subject.

  I was totally out of my body. Every few minutes.
  Every half hour. Every once in a while. Every
  morning. Every afternoon. Every day.
  Every night. Every other day. Every
  week. Every weekend. Every month.
  Every year. Every evening. Every time.

Let me give you a little backstory. Memories from childhood.
In our house, dinner was twenty minutes and done and often
  on TV trays.

Nobody talked to me.
Nobody gave me money.
Nobody told me their story.

Nobody laughed.
Nobody spoke.

To me, being Jewish just meant otherness.
There are three kinds of Jews:
Orthodox Jews, who only read Hebrew;
Conservative Jews, who read Hebrew and
English; and Reform Jews, whose only
requirement is to sing show tunes.

There are rites of passages.

Garry was the first of three.
Mitch Hurwitz and Jill Soloway
are the other two.

Garry was my dear friend, my teacher.
That Garry Shandling. My friend, Garry Shandling.
Garry would teach me about spontaneity.
Garry redesigned the wheel of comedy.
Garry had some serious chops.
Garry broke the fourth wall, addressed
the viewers.
Garry came up with the idea for a kind of
meta fake talk show.

The great Mitch Hurwitz has this beatific,
winning smile.
The first thing you notice about Mitch
is that he has a big gorgeous face
topped by a huge forehead. I
honestly think he has two brains.
Mitch isn't afraid to be completely silly.
Mitch told me about this family called
the Bluths.

Here comes our Jill. Jill whispered because
Jill fearlessly didn't yell.
Jill's eyes. They shine and go deep.
There is just no doubt that she is a seer.
Jill Soloway has "attaboy" in her DNA.
Praise is the heart and soul of Jill.
Jill has the lightest and yet deepest touch.
I was nigh on seventy years old when

Jill Soloway bestowed Maura Pfefferman
of *Transparent* on me.

Are you anybody?

This is who I am...

I make my bed every morning.
I love making my bed.
I am that boy.
I am an authority on fear.
I am in awe of teachers.
I am averse to friends and business.
I am alive because of daydreaming.
I am incapable of telling a joke.
I am forever grateful.
I am consumed by why
people *stop*.
I am a cisgender male.
I am known for walking into
women's bathrooms in airports.
I am the first person to say
the c-word on television.

I am the last Tambor standing.
I am an actor. That's who I am.

Hey now!

From *Are You Anybody?* Jeffrey Tambor, Crown Publishing, 2017.

I never got to write the come-to-Jesus scene I planned.

MY LIFE TO LIVE

I was named after my mother   my single   working mother
because my father rejected me   I always felt inferior
        not sure if it's a gift or a curse
accustomed to mother's daily departures   I was still lonely
        stalled in that limbo   I sought comfort

MY CHERISHED PAPER DOLLS

these were not conventional paper dolls   cut outs
the source of my dolls was the daily comics   funny papers
        lifelike   because of their mobility
my own paper dolls   I cut out   to make up stories

in my make-believe world   new characters were created
        real people   with problems
my star paper doll   a femme fatale   who got what she wanted

NUNS AND DOORS

attended a parochial school   skipped from second to third grade
        taught by Dominican nuns
        overwhelmed   by the most minute incident
        escalated into lifelong trauma   myriad behavior problems
        (does school teach that?)

THE TRAUMA OF MY SHATTERED FAMILY

as a child   dialogue and plot lines
        for my paper dolls   swirled   in my head
        story line   the subject matter of a soap opera
a large number of interconnected characters
        the plot unspooled   naturally

story   built through many vicissitudes   and heartrending separations

COMING EVENTS CAST THEIR SHADOW

I made it a practice to be more reflective about everything
to describe experiences I'd had in my own personal life

father's death had a dramatic effect on my writing style

judge my narrative bent different from that of the other serial dramas

I DEVISED A COMPLICATED FILING
I took several of grandmother's discarded telephone books
began cataloging my dolls by the names I'd given them

a separate phone book formed a sub-file
according to the clothes they wore their physical positions
standing sitting walking running
even dancing if the comic-strip artist drew such a figure

I created one doll whose father went to work
but would be gone for days
that doll asked me why don't you have a father?
then the doll said you don't have a father because he doesn't love you

LOCATIONS
at the funeral parlor I was just a bewildered little girl
frightened by coming face-to-face with death

a dollar store now fills the lot where grandmother's home once stood

an entire Connecticut warehouse is filled with
tens of thousands of my scripts

CREATE DRAMATIC TENSION
so many people tried to stand in my way
I was able to continue writing creating characters
inventing stories

THE TRAGEDY THAT BESET HUMANKIND
interpersonal conflicts jealousy hate love or avarice
characters who were born innocent but
through tragic circumstances were rendered evil

BRINGING MY DIALOGUE TO LIFE
inseparable   from my Dictaphone
I had to get my ideas down   whenever   wherever inspiration struck
I never tired of writing   the real world of make believe

CALLED A SOAP OPERA
because its audience was largely female
    its sponsors made products used in washing
every individual's life   has a soap opera in it
    unlike many TV stories

THE CHOICE FOR DAYTIME TV
living in my real world   of make-believe
    I created   backstories   for my show

it was a great joy to see   such talent   gathered in the room
    talent that was devoted   to my real world of make-believe

all those years of playing with those   damn paper dolls
    finally paid off   on the air

I wanted to create   not only to entertain
I was compelled to create
    to help people better understand   themselves

AUNT EMMA, THE GOSPEL TRUTH
Aunt Emma   read the comics to me
    I didn't find the stories   absorbing
sometimes she offered what she thought the characters
    might do   or become   and those ideas caught fire with me

Aunt Emma   confided in me   her desire   to be a writer
she took correspondence courses   in creative writing
    never had anything published   but she had grace

Aunt Emma was born   with one leg much shorter than the other
she had to wear a painful leg brace   and hideous extension shoe
    even so   she walked with a limp   her entire life

Aunt Emma was our family's   private saint   not an exaggeration
    her motivation was to make   other people happy

she never complained

SOAPS NEVER GO ON HIATUS
The real world   never stops
        neither did my make-believe world

I feel a space in my brain   a room where writing ideas are born

I don't think of stories   I hear voices   people   in scenes
        talking to each other   speaking to me
my whole life   I've felt compelled   to put them on paper

FIVE SCRIPTS A WEEK
a plethora of plot twists   plus backstory   and some real basic sex
        these characters   a special make-believe world   on tv

life is a soap   the real world keeps coming   at you
I had no choice but to be   a writer   I loved every minute of it

---

From *My Life to Live* by Agnes Nixon. Crown Publishing, 2017.

THIS TIME TOGETHER

Never in my wildest fantasies
Could I have ever imagined
That one day I would have
My own show on TV.

Nanny raised me.
My mama's mama.
She is the one
I pull on my ear for
On television.

We were poor
But so was
Everyone else
In the neighborhood.

Yucca and Wilcox
One block north
Of Hollywood Boulevard
But a million miles
From Hollywood.

In audition mode—doing flips,
Jumping, tap-dancing to be noticed.

> Hello?
> Carol?
> This is Carol Burnett.
> It's Carol.
>
> Carol, where're you goin'?
>
> Carol Burnett busy ordering seconds
> Of knockwurst and wiener schnitzel...
>
> Well, gosh, Carol.
> Carol was there.
> Carol there as promised.
> In a tutu, tap dancing and
> Doing some baton twirling.

TA-DA! A huge clap of
Thunder. Applause!

(All in one breath) Well-Mr.-Foy-a-friend-of-mine-from-California-where-I-just-came-from-worked-with-you-in-a-movie-he-had-a-bit-part-as-an-Irish-cop-remember-anyhow-he-said-you-were-a-real-swell-guy-and-that-maybe-when-I-get-to-New York-I-should-ask-you-for-your-advice-on-how-to-get-into-show-business-I-can't-get-a-job-cause-I-don't-have-an-agent-and-I-can't-get-an-agent-unless-they-see-me-in-something!

Sometimes I daydream
About being young again.
Doing it all over again.
Doing what I love.

It's time to throw off the covers, Carol.

This is Carol.
Meet Carol.
Hey Carol!
Aren't you Carol Burnett?
Darling Carol.
Carol, darling.
Dear Carol.

Television came knocking.
CBS Television City.

Saturday night. Super ratings.
Ratings in the top ten.

Doing the opening questions and answers
For "The Carol Burnett Show" every week
I could always count on somebody asking
Me to do the Tarzan yell.

Actually, it's nothing more
Than a drawn out (and loud) yodel.

Our show has been
Accused of showing
Actors cracking up
At times. Guilty as
Charged. We really

Tried hard *not* to
Break up. When we did,
It was honest.

I had always wanted a chin.
I was born with a weak one.
Anyhow, now I had a chin.
Thanks to a surgeon in Honolulu.

Grinning ear to ear.
Belt it out—and I mean BELT it out!
I have a chin. YES! A new chin. Yes, yes!

This is Carol Burnett.

Laugher and Reflections: A Conversation with Carol,
Where the Audience Asks the Questions

Lights up.

...just raise your hands and here we go!

Carol: Soooo.
Carol: Y'Know.
Carol: Yep. Sure.
Carol: Yessireebob. Yep.
Carol: Uh.

Carol, you MUST listen to me.

Carol, if you could be a member of the opposite sex for twenty-four hours, and then pop back and be yourself again, who would you be and what would you do?

(Excuse me???)

Hey, Carol. What's up?
Carol Burnett is almost very pretty.
Carol Burnett's going to whip their ass.
Carol's doing this and Carol's doing that.
Carol's show.

Carol, go on and give
Her your autograph.

With love, Carol.

Tug on my ear for nanny.
A way of saying hello.
I love you.
Your check
Is on the way.

Carol, where do you want to be buried?

Excuse me but aren't you Carol Burnett?
Yes, I am.
I knew it! Do you know how I could tell?
No...
By your face.

We put on 280 shows.
Roughly 2,520 sketches
And musical numbers.

Television was my home.
Making television history
In Television City.

The final strains of
"I'm So Glad We Had
This Time Together."

I sang, "Comes the time we have
To say so long," pulled my ear
For the last time, and it was over.

From *This Time Together* by Carol Burnett. Random House, 2011.

JEANNIE OUT OF THE BOTTLE

— haiku —

censors banned me
from revealing my belly
button on TV!

From *Jeannie Out of the Bottle* by Barbara Eden. Crown Archetype, 2011.

I'm the guy who came on TV
late at night
to sell you a Veg-O-Matic
a Pocket Fisherman
or Mr. Microphone.
I'm Ron Popeil.
As seen on TV.

THE SALESMAN OF THE CENTURY

— an abridged index —

From *The Salesman of the Century* by Ron Popeil. Delacorte Press, 1995.

Product names and trademarks are used throughout this poem to describe, and inform the reader about, various products that are owned by third parties. No endorsement of the information contained in this poem is given by the owners of such products and trademarks, and no endorsement by the publisher is implied by the inclusion of products and trademarks in this poem.

LIFE IS NOT A REALITY SHOW

I am fortunate. I've always been fortunate. So fortunate to be doing a reality show. I don't always use foundation. In the daytime, I often just wear tinted sunblock, either Laura Mercier or Proactive. When I want more coverage, Make Up For Ever has a liquid foundation that's amazing. I never wanted to do a reality show. On TV, I just basically felt like I'd been pushed way down the totem pole. I was a child actress. I was naive in thinking that filming a reality show would be easy. We're miked (sic) at all time. Cameras are filming you living your life. When your emotions run away with you, you can totally forget you're being filmed. Since I became one of the *Real Housewives of Beverly Hills*, I have suffered. Suffered terrible anxiety. Panic attacks. If you're a working mom, you know exactly what I'm talking about. I face the same kind of dilemmas. I do the grocery shopping for my family. I know some people who never set foot inside a grocery store. I never let the housekeeper pack lunches for my kids. Always do it yourself. Keep it real. Ha-ha! Always mull over a radical change of hairstyle. Go to more than one hairdresser. Go to a wig store and try on the cuts and colors. Don't torture your hair. I don't believe in spending a lot of money on my hair. I absolutely swear by Pantene. I am not a paid spokesperson for Pantene. Though I should be. Ha-ha! I saw a commercial for it and tried it and I thought, it really is like the commercial—my hair looks good. Some women I know never do their own hair. Hand to God. One woman with whom I am aquatinted goes to the salon literally every day. Like some people go to the gym—every day! I won't lie. I can't lie. I couldn't lie. I'm popping Cheez-Its. Mom loved diamonds, cars, and furs. I saw my father on the weekends. My sisters married very well. Yes, Mauricio and I are very well-off. We're blessed. But we have nowhere near the wealth of many of the people we know. I am not made of money. I am a huge fan of L'Oreal Voluminous. Both the regular and original one in the grey tube, called voluminous Full-Definition, and the Carbon Black Voluminous version. *Real Housewives* has been quite an education. *Real Housewives* is quite challenging for me because it creates a lot of stress. The show centers around conflict. That's actually the whole point of the show! My daughters find the *Real Housewives* entertaining. I'm not only passionate, I'm also *com*-passionate. I don't think it came across in season one. I can be fierce. But that's only one aspect of my personality, not the majority of who I am. I have a gorgeous purple crystal geode on my dining room table—it's supposed to be good energy. I love being fresh and clean. I don't look paparazzi-ready every time I leave the house. But I do try to look pulled together. I use a magnifying mirror to get everything perfect. Oh my God, this show is aging me! I love Altoids. I was always hyper focused on my body. I am still focused on my body. Sometimes I give into my cravings for things like cheeseburgers and fries from Fatburger. My middle has always been my problem area. When low-rise jeans were all the rage, it was terrible for me. I know my flaws. It's a contradiction for me to criticize parts of my body. I've had four kids, and I've never had lipo. I'm very grateful to Miracle Bras and Spanx! One day I was wearing Spanx under my outfit and my skirt flew up a little bit. Alert the paparazzi. Children crave attention. They soak it up like a sponge. I am a fanatic about Christmas. We celebrate Christmas and Hanukkah at our house. Kwanza too. Fruity O's aren't Froot Loops. I buy Fruity O's and put them in a Froot Loops box. Fake it till you make it. That's what I tell my girls. You always want a man to think you have plenty going on in your life. Play a little bit hard-to-get. Only bullies and controlling types are drawn to individuals who advertise their poor self-esteem. Show a little less—a classy look will appeal to classy types of guys. Don't wear something that barely covers your ass and lets your boobs hang out. But don't be obvious. Always act like a lady. Being myself is something I do well. I'm Beverly Hills born and bred. All my life. I'm a strong person. I'm a control freak. I'm a perfectionist. Glamourous all the time! I am not lazy about my manicures and pedicures. I am definitely not your typical Beverly Hills mom. I really respect and admire women who have no choice but to work long hours away from their families, yet still manage to keep everyone and everything going. Some without a husband. I have it a lot easier than some mothers. I have friends who are having a hard time keeping food on the table right now. Weight Watcher bars are really good. Believe me, life is not like the movies. It's funny, I never thought of myself as a naive person. When you're not feelin' it, you just have to fake it! This is one of my favorite expressions. Who made me feel that I could accomplish anything if I set my mind to it? I wear a certain ring on my right hand all the time. I get a lot of questions about it on Twitter and Facebook. Starbucks Verona, one packet of Splenda. A huge amount of Coffee-mate. It has to be Coffee-mate. That powder takes coffee to a whole new level. Let's play a game! Put on a CD with peaceful sounds of the ocean and make everything as peaceful as possible. Let's think. I'll point you to products that I totally swear by—most of which you can buy at the drugstore. Colgate whitening toothpaste. L'Oreal Voluminous Full-Definition and Carbon Black Voluminous. Dermablend Professional Cover Creme. St. Ives with Royal Jelly. Make Up For Ever waterproof liner for the inside eyelid. Hashmi Kajal kohl eyeliner (available on eBay). You don't have to spend a lot of money to care for your looks. Experiment with different brands from the drugstore. Ha! I'm kidding. Look in the Yellow Pages under *beauty* and *makeup*. Or do an online search. Make Up For Ever HD Foundation. For blush: The Balm. Epicuren, Verabelle. Cetaphil. *Pafums des Calins, Lancome.* MAC (Satin Taupe). NARS (all colors). Andrea EyeQ's Make Up Remover Pads, Oil-Free and Ultra-Quick. It's you who's going to be wearing your face. Learn how to do your makeup *yourself.* Television can be okay. Some channels can be educational and help a child learn their ABCs or even life skills. Shows are supposed to serve as cautionary tales. If I could help one person, it would mean so much to me. I am not above using scare tactics with my kids. I cry laughing at some memories from growing up. How could they be so heartless? I used to go to K-Mart, and they had the machine air-popping the popcorn and the Icees. Target reminds me of when I was a little girl. Every year I go there and I take a picture of myself with my Blackberry. I walked around with two caterpillars over my eyes until I was twenty-five years old! Ha-ha! But don't overpluck your eyebrows! I am not one of those people that finds cooking relaxing. All the chopping and cooking. NOT GOOD! Sometimes I'm given to uncontrollable tears. I enjoy being a girl. I am the youngest of three sisters. Wait. Hello! Somebody tell me I'm wonderful! I'm a very open and honest person. Everyone who watches *Real Housewives of Beverly Hills*, or just *Real Housewives*, as I refer to it, knows that my family lives a comfortable life. You might assume that in real life all of us who live here sit around sipping champagne and getting our hair done when we're not lunching or limo-ing with other TV people. Sometimes it feels like there's no time to even breathe! I am touched easily and quite intensely by things. I am grateful for paparazzi at the grocery store. I am so genuinely attracted to my husband. I never flirt with people other than my husband. I am a very honest person. I cannot stand lying—liars make me insane. Thank God for the telephone! Thank God. Thank God for *not* giving me triple-D boobs. I don't want boobs that big! Ha! I am not a jealous person at all. I said yes to Lexapro. And thank God I did. Some people are open to seeing their flaws and will appreciate your honesty and thank you for pointing things out to them. I'm not a fan of all the plastic surgery. It doesn't make anybody look younger. You look the same age but with work done. I think old-school plastic surgery is fine, when an older woman gets a facelift. People have taken it to extremes. They're blowing up their faces. Come and walk the streets of Beverly Hills. You'll see. There's so much plastic surgery! So much bad plastic surgery. Is it really not okay to have laugh lines? I understand the appeal of fillers. I have used Botox. I am not going to be the only person in Beverly Hills with crows' feet. My favorite blush in the entire world is called The Balm. You can buy it online or in boutique makeup stores like Sephora. I won't spend $200 an ounce for a skin cream. Getting real suntans is just not my thing. Sunless Tanner. Tanning lotions by Clarin and Lancôme. Norell perfume. I have such a successful marriage. By Beverly Hill standards. The nicest car and the biggest house and the most attitude. Mauricio is such a nice guy. Being married is like taking care of a plant. We're blessed. Monetary blessings. I have small hands. I have never had to deal with infidelity. I have outgrown that behavior. Being a *real* housewife...being catty...avoiding drama...paparazzi lurking...playing it cool. So much drama. I never feel intimidated or insecure. And then, again, I just have to laugh. Ha-ha! And fashion. You know, I love it! CNN and *InStyle* magazine both named me one of the most stylish TV housewives. I adore clothes, handbags, shoes. Jewelry, hats, and so on. Chanel suits. Gucci jacket. The only flats I wear are Chanel. My big-ticket purchases tend to be handbags and shoes. The staples. Chanel and Gucci are obviously very high-end. Tight and sexy skirt. Cute short skirt Dolce & Gabana blazer. I love Saks, Barney's, and Neiman's. Neiman Marcus. $80 on a pair of leggings. Why? Why spend $80 for something you can get for $15? Everyone in Beverly Hills goes to Arturo Shoe Fixx. Prada peek-toe platforms in black leather. I need a good shoe. I am so addicted to heels. I am very hard on my shoes. I am all about handbags. I have great relationships. I have some single friends who are happy. And I have some single friends who worry. I have friends who have always been drawn to bad boys. Accessories are important. Jewelry. And don't forget sunglasses. H&M is a great place to shop for cheap but fabulous stuff. Another good place for nice, inexpensive stuff is Zara. I'm a huge fan of the designer Matthew Williamson. I have found three and only three brands of jeans that work for me: Paige, J Brand, and Adriano Goldschmied. Vanity and...my vanity. I get really close to the mirror. I prop up a book I just love, *Making Faces* by Kevyn Aucoin, who is a genius. I also bring a little spray bottle of Evian when I fly to spritz my face on the plane. My hair...well, I am totally neurotic about taking care of it. I am a brunette. I have to cover my gray. I have some tricks up my sleeve. Nice 'n Easy Root Touch-up by Clairol. Brazilian blowouts. Velcro rollers in my hair. Pantene works for me, and it doesn't cost a fortune. Pantene's conditioner. Shaper by Paul Mitchell. Shaper hair spray by Paul Mitchell. People assume I spend a ton of money on products—but I don't! My shampoo comes from a drugstore! K-Y Jelly. Hmm, yes. Ha-ha! (Just kidding!) Goody Ouchless hair elastics. People used to ask me about my extensions. Um. I don't have extensions. Never did. My niece Paris has her own line of hair extensions. When I see a really thin girl on a TV show, I make a point of saying, That girl is too thin; that's not attractive at all. I take responsibility for what comes out of my mouth on *Real Housewives*. The lip gloss I can't do without is L'Oreal Infallible in Sunset. My most beloved lip gloss ever is Trisha McEvoy Irresistible. It's really sparkly. I've worn it on the red carpet. I love that lip gloss. Some of my favorite lip glosses are inexpensive, like L'Oreal No. 8, Fairest Nude. Microdermabrasion? Easier to go barefaced if you have great skin. Some products make your skin look healthier and vibrant. Creams and lotions and potions. Wear moisturizer all day. My real secret: false lashes. I put individual lashes on the outer corners of my eyelids on top of my mascara. I buy Sita Lash Naturals Flare in medium black. Duo Eyelash Adhesive, dark tone. OMG! Oh my God. Copious amounts of eye cream. Bobbi Brown concealer under my eyes. Camouflage your flaws and highlight your assets. You have to be careful or you'll end up looking like a drag Queen. A little Visine. I am so tired. I always use Bobby Brown concealer under my eyes. People on Twitter and everywhere else say negative things about me. This is where the hummingbirds come in. I've had many strange things happen with hummingbirds. They linger close to me, flitting around outside the window of my kitchen, the Waldorf Astoria, the polo lounge at the Beverly Hills Hotel. We're at La Scala so much we call it the office! I love it when my husband opens the car door for me. But only when we're leaving—not when we arrive at our destination. Then I open the door myself because it's too embarrassing to sit there waiting. It may sound strange coming from someone who appears on a TV show, and in fact first appeared on a TV show when she was five years old, but I always thought of myself as quiet and shy. Are you happy now? Period. End of story.

From *Life Is Not a Reality Show: Keeping It Real with the Housewife Who Does It All* by Kyle Richards. HarperOne, 2011.

WHAT I KNOW FOR SURE

What I know for sure:	The light in your life comes in, one conscious breath at a time.
What I know for sure:	Every day brings a chance for you to draw in a breath, kick off your shoes, and step out and dance—to live free of regret and filled with as much joy, fun, and laughter as you can stand.
What I know for sure:	Pleasure is energy reciprocated: What you put out comes back. Your base level of pleasure is determined by how you view your whole life.
What I know for sure:	Gayle is a friend I can count on.
What I know for sure:	Reading opens you up.
What I know for sure:	The only way to endure is to adjust.
What I know for sure:	There is no strength without challenge, adversity, resistance, and often pain.
What I know for sure:	A lack of intimacy is not distance from someone else; it is disregard for yourself.
What I know for sure:	Everything happens for a reason.
What I know for sure:	Love is all around.
What I know for sure:	If you can survive eleven days in cramped quarters with a friend and come out laughing, your friendship is real.
What I know for sure:	Pets represent in our lives a connection to caring that's unconditional. And reciprocal.
What I know for sure:	There is no need to struggle with your body when you can make a loving and grateful peace with it.
What I know for sure:	Whatever you fear most has no power—it is your fear that has the power. The thing itself cannot

touch you. But your fear can rob you of your life. Each time you give in to it, you lose strength, while your fear gains it. That's why you must decide that no matter how difficult the path ahead seems, you will push past your anxiety and keep on stepping.

What I know for sure: You are built not to shrink down to less but to blossom into more. To be more splendid. To be more extraordinary. To use every moment to fill yourself up.

What I know for sure: Whatever your situation is right now, you have played a major role in creating it. With every experience, you build your life, thought by thought, choice by choice. And beneath each of those thoughts and choices lies your deepest intention. That's why, before I make any decision, I ask myself one critical question—What is my real intention?

What I know for sure: The most important adventure of our lives doesn't have to involve climbing the highest peak or trekking around the world. The biggest thrill you can ever achieve is to live the life of your dreams.

What I know for sure: Wealth is a tool that gives you choices—but it can't compensate for a life not fully lived, and it certainly can't create a sense of peace within you. Your dream may have nothing to do with tangible prosperity and everything to do with creating a life filled with joy, one with no regrets and a clear conscience. I've learned that the whole point of being alive is to become the person you were intended to be, to grow out of and into yourself again and again.

What I know for sure: If you peel back the layers of your life—the frenzy, the noise—stillness is waiting. That stillness is you. This is what I call a "glory, glory, hallelujah" moment. That moment is always available.

What I know for sure: It is an awesome gift to be alive on this beautiful planet. And I want my time here to be as bright as it can be.

What I know for sure:	The light in your life comes in, one conscious breath at a time. Breathe easy.
What I know for sure:	Your breath is your anchor, the gift you've been given—that we've all been given, to center ourselves in this very moment. Whenever I have an encounter that involves even the slightest tension, I stop, draw in a deep breath, and release. Nothing is more effective than a deep, slow inhale and release for surrendering what you can't control and focusing again on what's right in front of you.
What I know for sure:	Giving yourself time to *just be* is essential to fulfilling your mission as a human being.
What I know for sure:	Having the best things is no substitute for having the best life. When you can let go of the desire to acquire, you know you are really on your way.
What I know for sure:	How you spend your time defines who you are.
What I know for sure:	When you define yourself by the things you can acquire rather than see what you really need to be happy and fulfilled, you're not just living beyond your means or overextending yourself. You're living a lie.
What I know for sure:	Behind every catastrophe, there are great lessons to be learned.
What I know for sure:	The joy of learning well is the greatest reward.
What I know for sure:	A green minivan paused on the road and a young woman leaned out the window to yell, "You're the best teacher on TV!"

From *What I Know for Sure* by Oprah Winfrey. Flatiron Books, 2014.

ABOUT WILLIAM WALSH

William Walsh's books include *Questionstruck, Pathologies, Stephen King Stephen King, Ampersand, Mass., Unknown Arts* (all from Keyhole Press), *Without Wax* (Casperian Books), and *Forty-five American Boys* (Outpost 19).

www.ingramcontent.com/pod-product-compliance
Lightning Source LLC
LaVergne TN
LVHW080038170826
845677LV00025B/1459
9798218402297